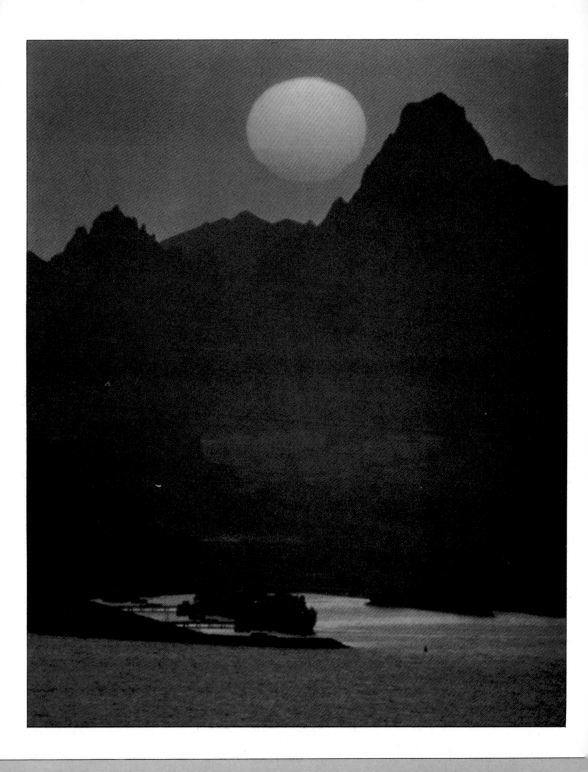

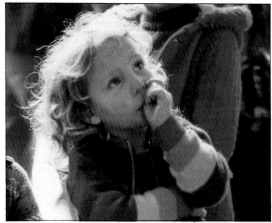

SLR
HANDBOOK

Series editor
Michael Langford

EBURY PRESS

The SLR Handbook was conceived, designed
and edited by **Dorling Kindersley Limited,** 9 Henrietta Street,
London WC2

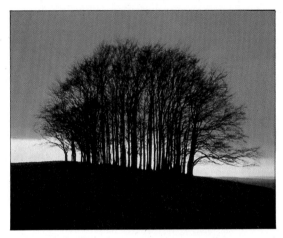

Technical adviser **Adrian Holloway**
Writer/researcher **Lucy Lidell**

Project editor **Joanna Godfrey Wood**
Art editor **David McGrail**
Designer **Debra Lee**
Assistant designer **Calvin Evans**
Managing editor **Joss Pearson**
Managing art editor **Stuart Jackman**
Editorial director **Christopher Davis**

Titles in the *Basic Photography Series* may share some common illustrations
where visual techniques shown apply to all photography and are not
restricted to specific equipment.

First published in Great Britain in 1980 by Ebury Press,
National Magazine House, 72 Broadwick Street,
London W1V 2BP

Copyright © 1980 by Dorling Kindersley Limited, London

ISBN 0 85223 171 7

Printed in the Netherlands by Smeets Offset B.V., Weert

Contents

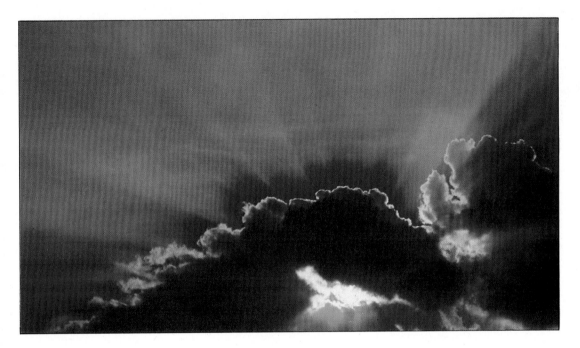

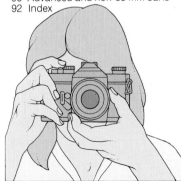

Introduction

This handbook is designed for people using single lens reflex (SLR) cameras. Since it is written mostly for first time owners, the book avoids advanced technical language and the most expensive equipment. Instead it concentrates on the essence of all good picture-taking: how to get the best out of your camera and avoid mistakes; how to take advantage of light, color, viewpoint and timing; and how to develop a photographer's eye for recognizing effective subjects.

Single lens reflex cameras are more accurate and versatile than other camera types. They allow you to view your subject through the actual taking lens, so that even working close up you always see exactly how much is included, and which parts are sharply focused. Most SLRs measure exposure through the lens too, which gives considerable accuracy and allows settings to be made automatically inside the camera. They also lead the way to more ambitious picture-making – for the lens is removable and you can fit others to give

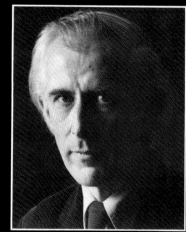

telephoto and wide angle effects. In fact your basic SLR camera body can be the start of a versatile system built up piece by piece as your hobby develops.

Used with today's films and flash equipment SLR cameras allow you to take pictures under almost any conditions. All the pictures in this book are attainable with a 35mm size single lens reflex, and although we concentrate on

this format the same principles apply both to 110 format and larger rollfilm size SLR cameras.

The first part of the handbook "Handling The Camera" (gray page borders) covers basic routines for handling your camera and taking pictures. The second section "Taking Better Pictures" (red borders) shows how to use composition and lighting, and gives practical advice on handling moving subjects, night shots, and taking flash pictures. The third section "Interpreting The Subject" (yellow borders), shows how to make the most of your photography with a whole range of popular subjects from weddings to foreign vacations. Finally the last section (gray borders) covers faults, accessories, advanced cameras and the presentation of your results.

Altogether the SLR Handbook will help give you better control of results and suggest new ideas for pictures. We hope it will encourage you to make fuller use of your camera and so increase your enjoyment of photography.
Michael Langford

Camera Basics
A **camera** is a light-tight box with a hole in the front covered by a lens. The **aperture**, adjustable in size, makes the hole larger or smaller, controlling the amount of light entering the camera. The **shutter** controls the time the light is allowed to act on the film.

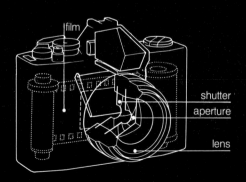

shutter
aperture
film
lens

The product of the combination of aperture and shutter is called **exposure**. The **lens** makes rays of light from the subject converge to form an image on the **film** (held flat in the back of the camera). An SLR **viewfinder** shows you the image formed by the lens as you compose the picture.

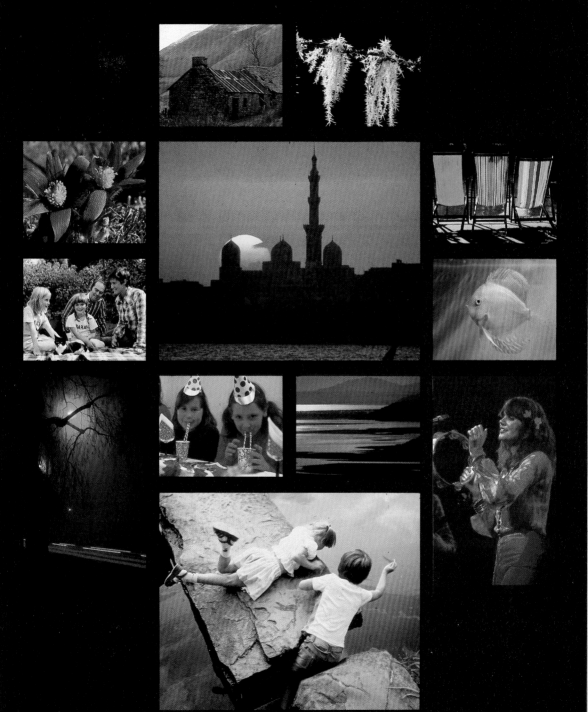

The basic SLR camera

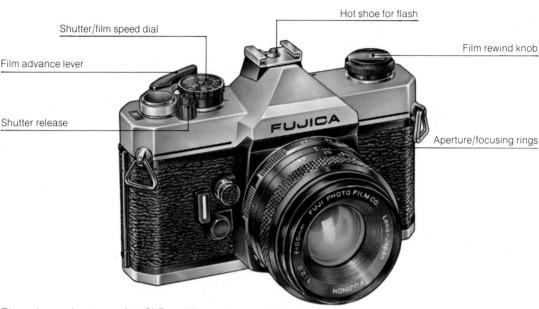

Shutter/film speed dial

Film advance lever

Shutter release

Hot shoe for flash

Film rewind knob

Aperture/focusing rings

FUJICA

The unique advantage of an SLR (single lens reflex) camera is its through-the-lens viewing system (p.10). This allows you not only to compose your shot in the viewfinder but also to see the effect of changing focus and aperture, or using a different lens or a filter for special effect. The wide range of interchangeable lenses and accessories for the 35 mm SLR makes it the most versatile camera available. A typical model, shown above, has a built-in exposure meter (p.13) and full-aperture focusing (p.12) for easier viewing. Other common features are shown below.

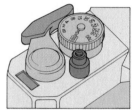

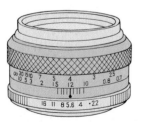

Lens
35 mm SLRs are generally sold with a standard (50 or 55 mm) lens, which can be interchanged easily (p.22). The lens barrel carries the focusing ring, the distance scale (p.11), the aperture control ring, and the depth of field scale (p.13).

Rewind knob/battery
The rewind knob opens the camera when raised and locks it shut when in position. The rewind crank folds out of the knob to wind the used film back into the cassette. The battery chamber unlocks with a small coin.

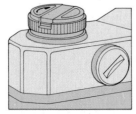

Self timer/preview button
The self timer enables you to include yourself in a picture (p.76). The preview button shows depth of field (p.13) at your selected aperture. On this camera it is combined with the exposure meter switch (p.19).

Film advance lever
This is used to wind the film forward one frame after you have pressed the shutter.
Film frame counter
This tells you how many pictures you have taken. It returns to "0" when the camera back is opened.
Shutter speed dial
This controls how long the shutter stays open (p.12). The selected shutter speed is usually indicated by a red line or dot.
Film speed dial
On this camera, the film and shutter speed dials are combined. You set the dial (p.17) to the ASA number of the film you are using.

35 mm film

35 mm film is packed in light-tight cassettes. Its image size (24 × 36 mm) allows full album page enlargement without loss of detail. There are three main types of 35 mm film on the market – for color prints, color slides, and black and white prints. Each is available in a wide variety of speeds, as shown by the chart below. The difference between the various film speeds is explained on p.16.

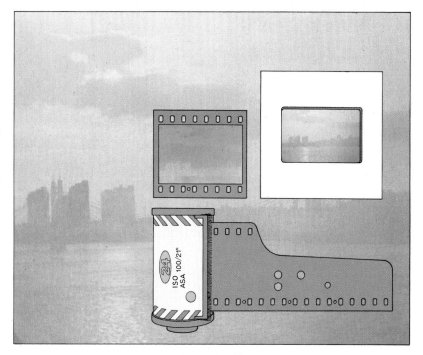

ASA	Color print	Color slide	B/W
25		•	
32			•
50		•	
64		•	
80	•		
100	•	•	
125			•
160		•	
200		•	
400	•	•	•
1250			•

Loading and unloading

35 mm film is relatively quick and simple to load, once you have had a little practice. Some cameras have an easy-load system, but most load according to the method shown in the diagrams right. Always load and unload film in the shade. And, when the film is finished, don't open the camera back until you have rewound it back into its cassette.

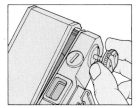

1 Hold the camera firmly and open the back by pulling up the rewind knob. The door will spring open.

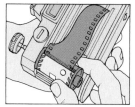

2 Keeping the rewind knob raised, put the cassette in the left chamber. Then push down the knob, turning it until it clicks home.

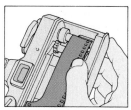

3 Pull the film leader tongue out and insert it in the take-up spool, the bottom row of perforations engaged on the sprockets.

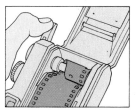

4 Alternately depress the shutter and wind on the film, until both rows of perforations engage the sprockets.

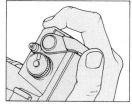

5 Close the camera back, and continue advancing the film until "1" appears in the exposure counter window. Now set the ASA.

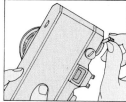

6 To unload, release the rewind button and turn the rewind crank clockwise until it goes slack. Open the camera and remove the film.

Viewing and focusing

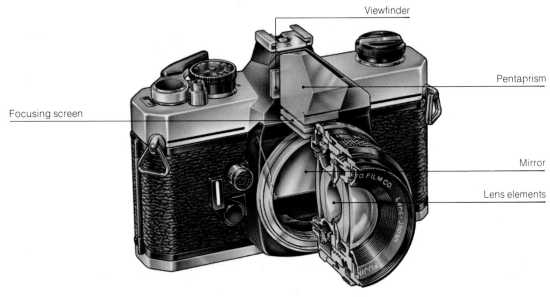

Viewfinder

Pentaprism

Focusing screen

Mirror

Lens elements

An SLR camera uses the same lens for viewing and taking the picture – hence its name "single lens reflex". Its unique design enables you to see through the viewfinder exactly what will be recorded on film, permitting the utmost accuracy of framing and focusing. This is achieved by a complex optical system, consisting of a mirror, a pentaprism, and various lens components (see below). When you press the shutter, the mirror flips up, allowing light to reach the film and temporarily blocking out your view. This is hardly noticeable at fast shutter speeds.

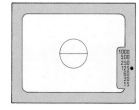

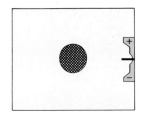

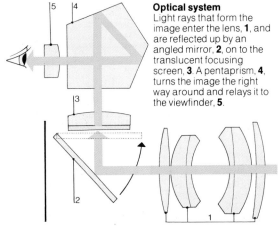

Optical system
Light rays that form the image enter the lens, **1**, and are reflected up by an angled mirror, **2**, on to the translucent focusing screen, **3**. A pentaprism, **4**, turns the image the right way around and relays it to the viewfinder, **5**.

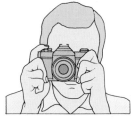

Viewing your subject
The viewfinder is the main information source of an SLR. It enables you to compose, set exposure, and focus without taking the camera away from your eye. When framing a shot, check that you can see all four sides of the viewfinder.

Typical SLR viewfinders either show a split image, top, or a microprism, above, in the central area of the focusing screen. They also display exposure data – the simplest by means of a centering needle, as above. Others show aperture and shutter settings, as top.

Focusing the lens

SLR cameras have a focusing ring on the lens barrel, which you turn to bring your subject into focus. Rotating the ring moves the lens closer to the film plane for distant subjects, farther away for closer subjects. To focus a picture, look through the viewfinder and turn the ring until your main subject looks sharp. The distance scale on the ring shows the focusing range of the lens – from a minimum distance to infinity (∞). To focus quickly, gauge the camera-to-subject distance and set it on this scale.

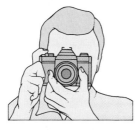
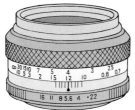

Subject distance and depth of field

When you focus, part of your image, both in front of and behind the subject, will be sharp. This zone of sharpness or "depth of field" varies according to the camera-to-subject distance. It is very limited close up but increases rapidly as you move farther away from your subject, as shown by the sequence right. To find out how much of your subject will be sharp, check on the depth of field scale. Depth of field is also affected by the size of the aperture (p.12) – these shots were all taken at f8.

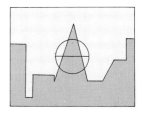

Finding sharp focus

On an SLR, the image over the whole focusing screen becomes sharper or fuzzier when you focus the lens. To help you to focus on a specific part of your subject, many screens incorporate a split-image finder in the center. When out of focus, the image in this area appears broken, as shown above left. When accurately focused, the two halves of the image converge into one, as above.

● Always focus on the part of the subject that is the most important.

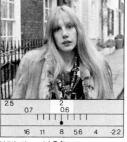

With the girl 2 ft away from the camera (the minimum focusing distance of the lens), depth of field is very limited – both the foreground and background are unsharp.

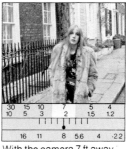

With the camera 7 ft away, the railings and window nearest the girl have come into focus. Depth of field extends from almost 6 ft to 9 ft.

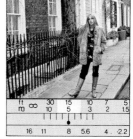

With the camera 15 ft away, the whole picture is sharp. Most standard lenses allow maximum depth of field at this distance. Use the ∞ setting only if you want the foreground out of focus.

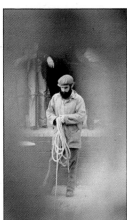

Focusing for effect

Sometimes it is more effective to blur part of your image, to give your shot emphasis and depth. Shooting with foreground elements closer than the minimum focusing distance creates a soft frame for the sharply focused figure, left. Alternatively, you can "defocus", or deliberately put your whole image out of focus, as right. Defocusing softens colors, spreads highlights into circular shapes and adds atmosphere to a shot. It is best used with strong, simple shapes (backlit scenes and silhouettes).

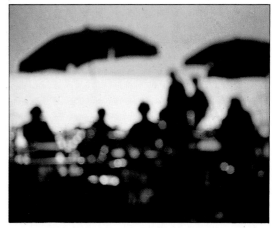

Controlling aperture and shutter

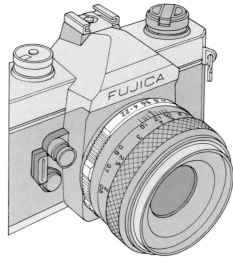

Aperture and shutter speed together determine exposure – how much light reaches your film (aperture) for how long (shutter). Different combinations can give the same exposure. By varying shutter speed, you can control how moving subjects record: fast shutter speeds (brief exposure) freeze movement to a sharp image; slow ones (long exposure) let it blur. By varying aperture, you can alter "depth of field" – the amount of a scene that will be sharp in front of and behind the subject you focus on, see below. Most cameras have full aperture focusing – the aperture stops down as you press the shutter.

f	2	2.2	2.8	4	5.6	8	11	16	22	
	1000	700	500	250	125	60	30	15	8	4	2	B

Aperture/shutter scales
The aperture ring on the lens is marked in f numbers or "stops" from about f2 (open) to f16 ("stopped down"). The scale applies to all lenses, but the maximum aperture varies, and may not be a normal stop (here it is f2.2). The shutter dial is marked in seconds, from 1/1000 sec (fast) to 1/2 sec or longer, plus a B setting, on which the shutter stays open while the release is pressed. Each step on each scale halves or doubles the exposure. The scales are given in full, left, arranged so each pair of settings gives the same exposure.

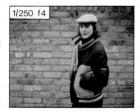
1/250 f4

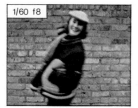
1/60 f8

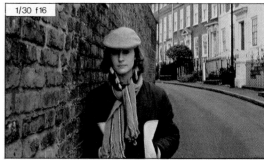
1/30 f16

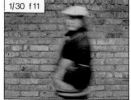
1/30 f11

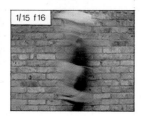
1/15 f16

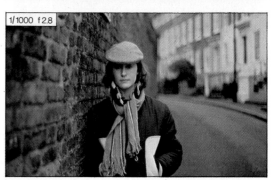
1/1000 f2.8

Shutter speed and motion
The four pictures above all received the same exposure, but at different aperture and shutter settings. The effect of shutter speed shows in the moving figure – sharp at 1/250 sec and increasingly blurred at the slower speeds.

Aperture and sharpness
The two pictures right also received the same exposure, but at extremes of aperture. With the lens stopped down, top, sharpness extends throughout the picture. At wide aperture, bottom, depth of field is shallow – only the subject is sharp.

Setting the controls

Decide which setting is most critical. If the scene contains movement, set the shutter speed first, right. If depth of field matters, set the aperture first, as below right. Then activate the meter (using the switch, button, or film advance) and look through the viewfinder as you adjust the second control. (Or set it to "A", for automatic.) When the displays show correct exposure, check the second setting to see how it will affect your picture – watch out for slow shutter speeds, and re-adjust the controls if this is necessary.

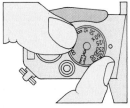

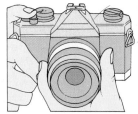

Using the displays

Manual cameras allow you to adjust both controls, and usually display a needle which you must center between + and – signs. Semi-automatic cameras set one control, while you adjust the other. They often display the automatic setting in the viewfinder – with a moving light on a shutter speed scale, or an aperture read-out window. In practice, this allows you to control the automatic setting as well as the manual one. Simply adjust the manual setting until the displays show the desired automatic setting.

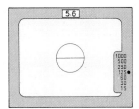

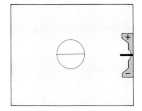

Depth of field scale

You can also judge depth of field from the scale on the lens. This shows a series of lines, colored (or numbered) in pairs to match your f numbers. Each pair marks off on the distance scale the depth of field at one f stop. The lenses, left, show focus set at 7 ft (2 m). At f4 (red lines), depth of field is slight. At f16 (blue lines) it runs from 5 ft to 10 ft.

Depth of field depends on:
- **Focused distance:** least, close up; most, over 15 ft
- **Aperture:** least at low f numbers; most at high ones
- **Lens type** (p.22): least, telephoto; most, wide-angle

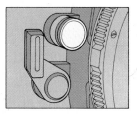

Aperture preview

As you set the controls, the aperture stays open. You see a bright image, with shallow depth of field, top right. To see the true depth of field, use the preview button, above. The lens will close to the aperture set, darkening the image, right.

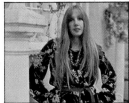

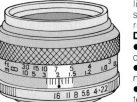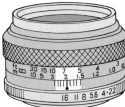

Using aperture and shutter creatively

Shooting at wide aperture allows you to make use of selective focusing. The shallow depth of field will render most of the foreground and background out of focus, effectively isolating the main subject, as left. This technique is useful with cluttered or crowded scenes, candid shots, small subjects, or ugly backgrounds. You must focus very carefully. The shot of a brass band, right, shows a creative use of slow shutter speed with camera jog (p. 31) for an abstract effect.

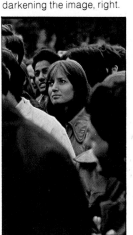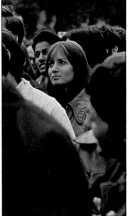

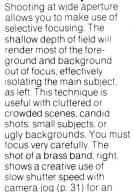

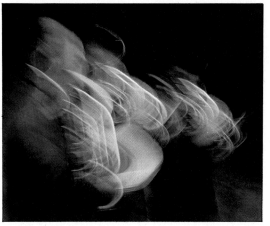

Supporting the camera

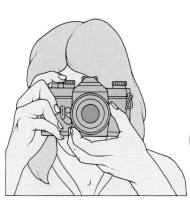

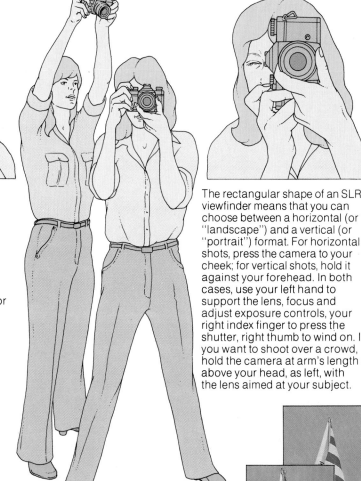

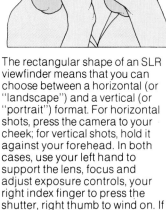

To take sharp pictures, you must hold your camera still. Support it with both hands in a steady but relaxed grip and tuck your arms in. Stand firmly with your legs apart and your weight evenly distributed. Then hold your breath or breathe out slowly as you press the shutter. Keep the camera strap around your neck or wound around your wrist to keep it secure. Before using a new camera, practice raising it to your eye, setting the controls, pressing the shutter and winding on until your actions are familiar and smooth.

The rectangular shape of an SLR viewfinder means that you can choose between a horizontal (or "landscape") and a vertical (or "portrait") format. For horizontal shots, press the camera to your cheek; for vertical shots, hold it against your forehead. In both cases, use your left hand to support the lens, focus and adjust exposure controls, your right index finger to press the shutter, right thumb to wind on. If you want to shoot over a crowd, hold the camera at arm's length above your head, as left, with the lens aimed at your subject.

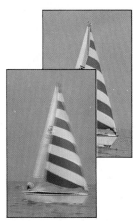

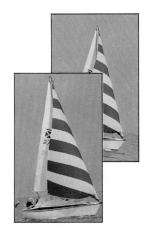

Avoiding shake
Blurred pictures are more often caused by camera shake than inaccurate focusing. To avoid jogging the camera, hold it firmly, as shown above, and support it if you are using shutter speeds below 1/60 sec (see facing page).

Pressing the shutter
If you jab the shutter release, you may push down one side of the camera, and cause crooked horizontals and verticals, as right. Always press the shutter gently, with the cushion, not the tip, of your finger.

Shooting positions

You will find it far easier to hold your camera steady if you look for a way of supporting your body. For a normal, eye-level viewpoint, lean your body against something solid, such as a fence, tree, lamp post or wall, as shown right. When taking children, pets or small animals, you should get down to their level. Either sit with your legs crossed and your elbows on your knees, as shown below right, or rest your elbows on a low, flat surface. Don't squat – it is too difficult to keep your balance. For really low viewpoints, lie full length on the ground, and support your weight on your elbows.

Slow shutter speeds

When using shutter speeds slower than 1/60 sec (or 1/125 sec with a telephoto lens), you must support the camera. If you don't have a tripod, rest the camera on a flat surface or hold it vertically against a wall, as shown right. Use a soft cloth or handkerchief to protect the lens barrel from scratches. A tripod offers maximum stability for long exposures. Tripods screw into the base of the camera and most have extendible legs to enable you to shoot from different heights. Avoid touching the camera during exposure by using a cable release or the self timer to fire the shutter.

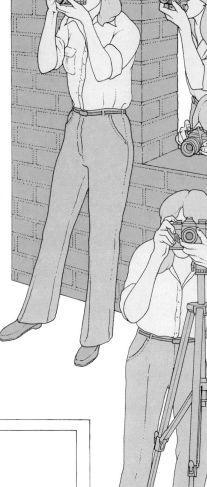

Avoid touching the camera

During a long exposure, you should avoid all contact with the camera by using a cable release or self timer. A cable release screws into the shutter release button and allows you to fire the shutter from a distance. Cocking the camera's self timer releases the shutter after a delay of several seconds, giving you time to move away from the camera (p.76).

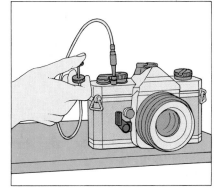

Film types and speeds

There is a wide variety of films on the market, but deciding which one to use should not be a problem. The main things to consider are: do you want color prints, slides or black and white? Will you be shooting in dim or bright light? Do you prefer a particular color effect? For example, Ektachrome is bluer and Kodachrome is redder. It all depends what kind of shots you want to take. When you find a film you like, stick to it most of the time, changing only for a special reason.

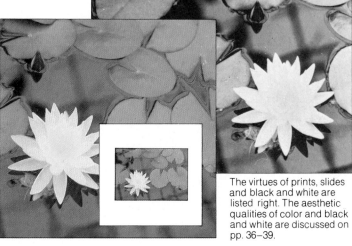

The virtues of prints, slides and black and white are listed right. The aesthetic qualities of color and black and white are discussed on pp. 36–39.

Buying a film
When you go to buy a film it will help if you can interpret the coding on the pack.

Check the following points:
● Size – 135 (for 35 mm film cassettes)
● Type – color print, color slide or black and white; suitable for daylight/flash or tungsten light (see facing page)

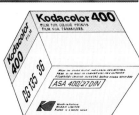

● Speed – ASA/DIN/ISO numbers (see "Setting the ASA", facing page)
● Number of exposures – normally 20 or 36
● Expiry date
● Whether the price includes processing

Film speed
A film is given an ASA (DIN/ISO) number to show how sensitive it is to light. The higher the number, the more sensitive it is and the faster it reacts to light. Fast film therefore requires less light to take a picture. For most daylight shots use a medium speed film (64 to 125 ASA), but for dim light use a faster film (200 to 400 ASA for color, 400 ASA and over for black and white). For really poor lighting conditions, uprate the film. You can get very slow film for slides (25 to 50 ASA) and black and white prints (32 ASA).

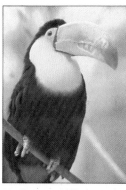

Medium speed film is used for general purpose photography in normal daylight or bright lighting.

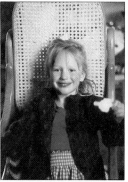

Fast film is used for dim light, interiors, dusk, fast action, and distant flash photographs.

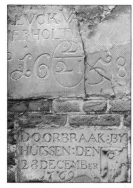

Slow film is used for close-up work, still life, and very brightly lit scenes. It gives fine detail and rich colors.

Setting the ASA
After loading your camera, set the ASA dial, bottom right, to match the film speed. The ASA number is marked on the film cassette, top right, but it cannot be seen once the camera back is closed. Try sticking the relevant part of the film pack on to the camera back to remind you of the number. Check regularly that the dial has not slipped round to another number.

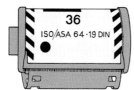

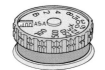

If you notice that the ASA dial has slipped off the correct setting:
1 Shoot the rest of the film at the same setting.
2 Make a note of the wrong setting.
3 Enclose a note to your processor stating the incorrect ASA number and asking for your shots to be corrected. Check with your retailer for the name of a laboratory offering this service.

Uprating the film
Where lighting conditions are too dim to allow you a fast enough shutter speed or a small enough aperture for your subject, you can obtain a higher speed from your film by "uprating". Set the ASA dial at up to three times the proper film speed and be sure to tell the laboratory so that they can give extra processing to your film to compensate.

Which film?
Most people use color prints for convenience – you can look at them easily, display them in albums or frames, and have them duplicated. But if you invest in a good projector and screen, slides offer brilliant color, greater realism and the pleasure of an evening slide show. Black and white films are cheaper, fun to experiment with and easy for home darkroom work. You may do best to use a mixture: color prints to record family events and to send copies to friends; black and white to experiment with new picture ideas; slides to illustrate a special vacation. Besides the three basic film types, there is a variety of films available for special effects, such as infra-red film and high-contrast line film. Be sure you always use fresh film and have your pictures processed promptly.

	Prints	Slides	Black and white
Cost	● Most expensive	● Cheaper per shot	● Cheapest
Quality	● Realistic; fair color and sharpness	● Extremely realistic; brilliant color	● Less realistic; more abstract; fine detail, wide tonal range
Viewing and storing	● Easy in albums and frames	● Projector and storage system necessary as slides are easily damaged	● Easy in albums and frames
Duplicating and enlarging	● Easy; can be cropped, framed, etc	● More expensive to have prints made. Duplicates of slides lose quality	● Very cheap to duplicate and enlarge; easy for home darkroom work
Type of light	● Gives accurate color in most lighting except fluorescent	● Accurate color with daylight or flash; avoid room lights (or use "tungsten" film or a filter)	● Any light
Exposure errors	● Less likely to show errors as prints are given some correction	● Extra care must be taken with exposure	● Least likely to show errors as it is easiest to correct during printing
Speeds	● Only two generally available; medium (80 to 100 ASA), or very fast (400 ASA)	● Wide range of speeds available, from 25 to 400 ASA	● Wide range of speeds available, from slow (32 ASA) up to ultrafast (1200 ASA) for low light conditions.

Color accuracy of films
Most color slide films are designed for use with daylight or flash. If they are used in artificial light or unusual lighting conditions, you will get a color cast. To correct the lighting balance, you must either use a filter or tungsten light film. With color negative film, casts are eliminated during processing and printing.

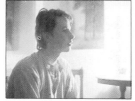
Yellow/red cast
Cause: domestic lamps. Use 82A, B or C filter, or try tungsten film.

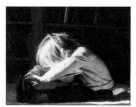
Blue cast
Cause: snow, dusk, deep shade under blue sky. Use 81A, B or C filter.

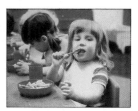
Green cast
Cause: fluorescent lighting. Use Kodak's FL-W filter.

Understanding exposure

SLRs use a variety of systems to help you with exposure: built-in meters; needles, scales or "LEDs" (lights) in the viewfinder; even automatic control. If the subject is lit evenly, from the front, and of even tone, these work well. But in uneven lighting, with strong bright and dark areas, you have to take care. Results will depend on where you direct the camera as it reads the subject. Learn to recognize different lighting, and when to choose a highlight reading, or a shadow reading, or an average between the two. If in doubt, err toward under-exposure with slides, and over-exposure with prints.

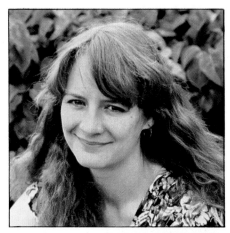

Correct exposure
A well exposed shot should look crisp, with detail in main areas, depth of color and tone, and bright but not bleached highlights, as left. Make sure the needle is level in the center (or displays are correct) and read from the area of main interest.

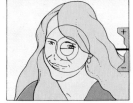

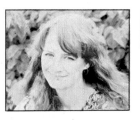

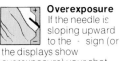
Overexposure
If the needle is sloping upward to the - sign (or the displays show overexposure) your shot will be pale, with bleached highlights, weak color, and indistinct detail. The shot left is 2 stops over.

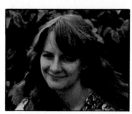

Underexposure
If the needle is pointing down to the sign, or the displays show under-exposure, your shot will be dark, with deep colors, and lack detail in shadows. The face left has turned deep orange (under by 2 stops).

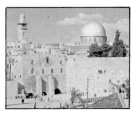

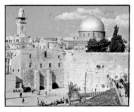

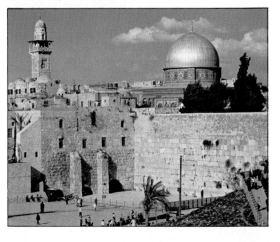

Bracketing
In uncertain lighting, or when you must be sure of a good result, it is wise to "bracket" exposure. This means taking extra shots at exposures close to the one your meter shows. Bracket by I stop each way – more in contrasty lighting. The

meter showed correct exposure for this scene at f11 on 1/60 sec, above center. At 1 stop over (1/30 sec), above left, there is more shadow detail, but highlights are burned out. Perhaps the most satisfying result is at 1 stop under (1/125 sec) as shown right.

Metering systems

Most SLRs have through-the-lens (TTL) metering, using light-sensitive cells to measure image brightness. The position of the cells determines the metering system, see right. No system is infallible – spot and center-weighted readings may be inaccurate if the subject is not centered; overall readings can be thrown off by uneven tones.

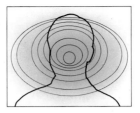

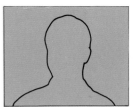

Spot system

Reads exposure from a small central area. Works well if spot is typical of scene.

Center-weighted system

Reads exposure from the whole scene, with increased sensitivity at the center.

Overall system

Reads overall brightness of picture area. Works best if tones evenly balanced.

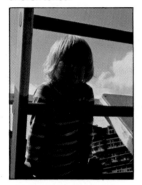

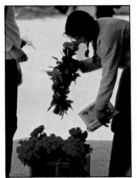

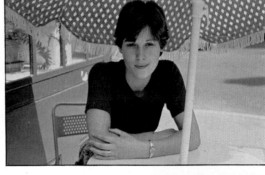

Contrasty light conditions

Uneven lighting may mislead any metering system. Dark or shaded subjects set against a light background or backlit, will be under-exposed, above. Subjects at the side of the frame, in a different tone to the center, will fool spot and center-weighted systems, above center. Subjects in different lighting from the camera, above right, mislead most systems. The solution to these problems is to go up close and *read exposure from the main subject*, right. Or read it from your hand, held in similar lighting.

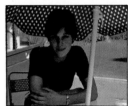

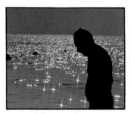

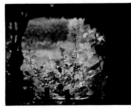

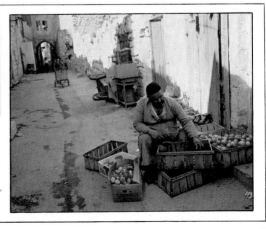

Selective exposure

You may get a stronger picture if you take a selective reading, from highlights or shadows only. (To get detail in both, take an average – but the result may be boring.) Exposing for highlights, above, has silhouetted the figure against the sea, and set the garden in a dark frame. Reading for shadows, right, has softened color and revealed detail.

Choosing and controlling flash

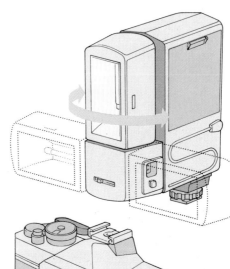

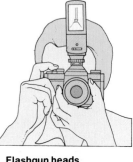

Flash can solve many problems. It matches daylight, so you can shoot anywhere on daylight film without the color casts you get with other lighting. In dim light, you can avoid wide apertures or long exposures with a tripod. And the brief flash – often equivalent to a shutter speed of 1/1000 sec – determines the length of the exposure, so you can freeze fast action. You can also use flash for special effects (p.31). Electronic flash is much more useful than bulbs, and cheaper in the long run. A model you can use off camera, preferably an automatic gun (facing page), is best.

Flashgun heads
The simplest guns have a fixed head, above. Costlier guns have a swivel head to alter flash direction, left, or a tilt head (for bounced flash, p.35). A few models can vary the beam width to suit your lens; others accept an attachment for telephoto.

Shutter speed for flash
With an SLR, you can only use certain shutter speeds for flash. The X, or red dot, on your shutter dial, left, marks the X synch speed for electronic guns. You can use slower shutter speeds. But never set a faster speed – your shot will be spoiled.

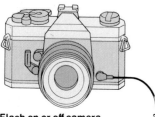

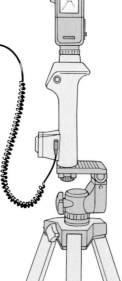

Flash on or off camera
Cordless guns are designed for use on the camera. They simply fit into the hot shoe, which synchronizes the flash and shutter firing. Most guns, however, have a cable which you plug into the X synch socket beside your lens, above. They can be used on the hot shoe, or off the camera. On-camera flash gives harsh and unflattering results. It is better to buy a model you can use off the hot shoe, perhaps with a grip handle and cable, right. You can use it on a tripod or stand, clamp it to the camera, or hold it where you wish.

Flash firing rate
Switch the gun on, and wait for the ready light to glow, above. Check the interval between firings before you buy a gun – long waits are annoying, and you may want to use the flash with an autowind (p.89). Renew the batteries if the rate slows.

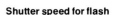

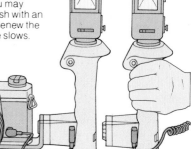

Controlling flash

Flash illumination falls off sharply, so subjects farther away get less light, and require greater exposure. If your gun is not automatic, you must adjust exposure yourself by selecting the right aperture. Most guns have a scale to help you, but some use "guide numbers" – divide the guide number for your film by the flash to subject distance, to get the required f stop. (For fill-in, p.35, use one f stop higher and set a shutter speed which gives correct daylight exposure – but don't exceed the X synch speed.)

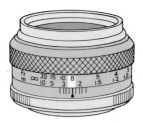

1 Judge flash distance
Set up your flash, using the X synch shutter speed and focus. With on-camera flash, you can read the subject/flash distance from your focusing ring. With off-camera, or bounced flash, estimate how far the light must travel.

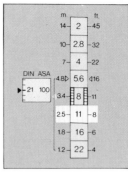

2 Use flashgun scale
Set your ASA on the scale, then read off the f no. for the subject/flash distance.

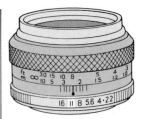

3 Set camera aperture
Set the aperture ring on the lens to the selected f number. If using flash in a confined, white-walled space, stop down by ½ to 1 stop. If diffusing it, open up by ½ stop. For very close subjects, it is always wise to diffuse the flash.

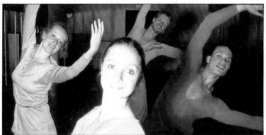

Flash fall-off
Flash cannot light subjects at different distances evenly, as above. Figures twice as far from the camera receive only one-quarter as much light, right.

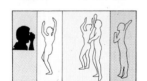

When using flash, make sure that important parts of your subject all lie at the same distance, right. Then lighting will be even, above. You can exploit fall-off to darken ugly backgrounds.

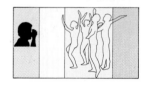

Automatic flashguns
More expensive, "computer-type" guns control flash exposure automatically, or have a manual/auto switch. Most are "self-quenching" guns – a light sensor on the gun reads light reflected from the subject, and cuts off the

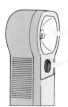
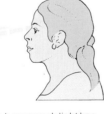

flash when enough light has been given. You may also be able to set the gun to give a briefer flash for fill-in shots. Automatic guns make flash photography simple, in most lighting situations (but for bounced flash, p. 35, you should switch to manual).

Flash faults
If you use a flashgun which gives a beam narrower than the view of your lens, you will get vignetting – dark, unexposed edges to the picture, as right. Here a wide-angle lens was used with a telephoto flash beam. If you set a shutter speed higher than that marked X on your dial, the result will be as shown below right. Half the frame is dark, because at high speeds an SLR shutter never clears the whole frame.

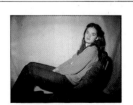
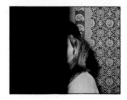

Using different lenses

On an SLR camera, you can remove your standard lens and replace it with another – wide-angle, to take in more of a scene and give three-dimensional depth; or telephoto, to enlarge a distant subject. Lenses are identified by "focal length" (the effective distance from lens to film, in mm) and speed (maximum aperture). Standard lenses are 50/55 mm, and fastest. Wide-angles range from 18 mm to 35 mm, telephotos from 80 mm to 500 mm, or more. A useful basic set of lenses is shown below. You can also choose from a range of more unusual lenses, including a zoom lens (p. 89).

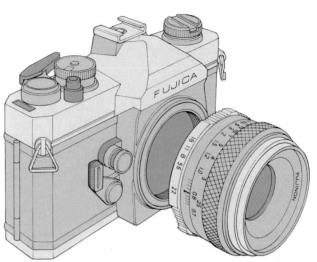

Buying a basic set
Adding a 28 mm wide-angle and a 135 mm telephoto to your normal lens gives you a basic set which will meet a wide range of situations. Buy the best you can, and check that the mount is compatible. Fast lenses allow higher shutter speeds.

The 135 mm telephoto lens
This moderate telephoto has a narrow angle of view, but magnifies the subject. It is useful for portraits, sports and wildlife. A telephoto is heavier than a standard lens so support it well at slow shutter speeds (below 1/125 sec).

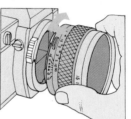

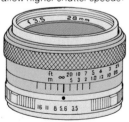

The 28 mm wide-angle lens
This medium wide-angle lens encompasses more of a scene than the standard lens. It is very useful for interiors, large groups, and panoramic views. It includes more of the foreground and gives depth, but avoids extreme distortion effects.

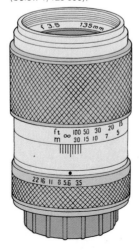

Bayonet mount
This is the quicker and more convenient method. You simply align the red dots on the lens and camera body and turn the lens until it clicks into place. On many models, you must depress a lens release lever before detaching the lens.

Adaptor mount
An adaptor mount, right, makes it possible for you to use a screw-mount lens on a bayonet-mount body, or vice versa. It also allows you to buy and use a lens designed by a different manufacturer to that of your camera body, if you wish.

Screw mount
Lenses with screw mounts are cheaper, but also less convenient. It is not always easy to align the grooves and, unless you take care, you can screw them in too far. Most 35 mm SLRs with a screw mount accept a 42 mm screw fitting.

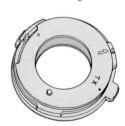

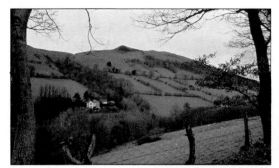

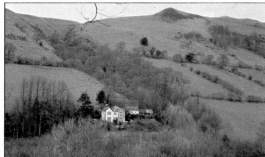

Using different lenses from the same viewpoint

Angle of view and image size both alter when you change lens. A 28 mm shot, above, distances the house but sets it effectively in its surroundings. A 50 mm shot, above right, draws the house in to the mid-distance but shows much less sky and foreground. A 135 mm shot, right, brings the house up close but eliminates the skyline and foreground altogether.

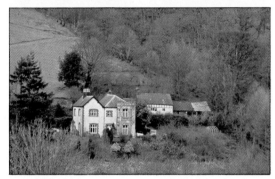

How lenses differ

A 28 mm, wide-angle lens:
- has a short focal length
- has a wide angle of view
- increases depth of field
- reduces subject size

A 50 mm standard lens:
- has a medium focal length
- gives an angle of view like that of the human eye
- has average depth of field

A 135 mm telephoto lens
- has a long focal length
- has a narrow angle of view
- reduces depth of field
- enlarges subject size

Using different lenses and changing viewpoint

The picture sequence, right, shows how you can alter the character and perspective of a scene radically, by changing both lens and viewpoint. Each time he changed his lens the photographer moved back to keep the wall of the house nearest to the camera at roughly the same size in the viewfinder frame.

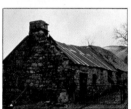

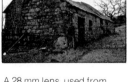

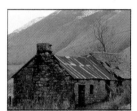

A 28 mm lens, used from a close viewpoint, distorts the shape of the nearest wall and makes the houses appear to recede sharply.

A 50 mm lens, used from farther back, shows the end wall in proportion and the row of houses in normal, eye-view perspective.

A 135 mm lens, used from even farther away, flattens perspective, making the row of houses look shorter and bringing the hillside close.

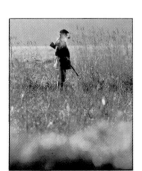

Lenses and depth of field

One of the main reasons for changing lens is to reduce or increase depth of field. A telephoto has little depth of field, a wide-angle extreme depth of field. If you want to isolate a subject from the setting, as left, use a telephoto lens at wide aperture. But if you want sharp detail from foreground to background, right, use a wide-angle lens, and stop down.

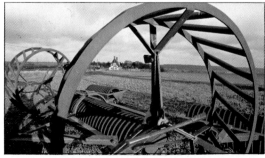

Before you press the shutter

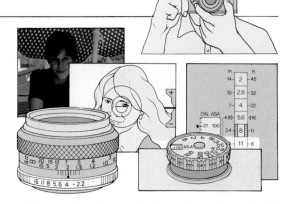

1 Set the exposure

- Have you set the ASA correctly for your film?
- Have you chosen the best aperture for depth of field and the best shutter speed for movement?
- Have you checked that the viewfinder displays show correct exposure?
- Have you switched on your flash gun, if required? (Remember the flash shutter speed and aperture for distance.)

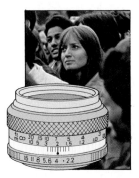
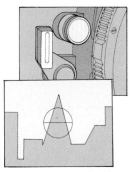

2 Focus accurately

- Have you focused on the most important part of your subject? (Make sure you are not closer than the minimum focusing distance.)
- Have you checked your depth of field – either by using the preview button or the depth of field scale?

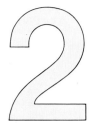
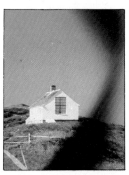

3 Check the viewfinder

- Have you made sure that you are not accidentally obscuring part of the lens with your camera strap, hair or fingers?
- Have you checked that horizontals and verticals are aligned with the edge of the frame?
- Have you provided support for the camera, if using a shutter speed below 1/30 sec?

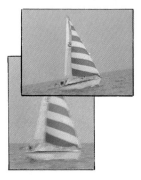
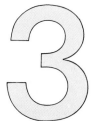
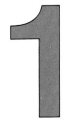

If the shutter won't press
Don't panic! It could be for one of the following reasons:

You have reached the end of the film

You have forgotten to wind on or have failed to wind on enough to cock the shutter

Your shutter lock (p.90) is in position

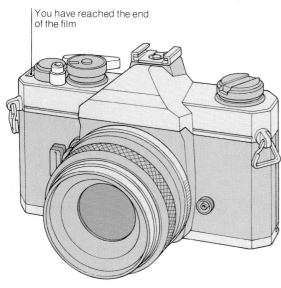

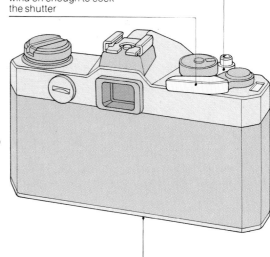

You have accidentally pressed the rewind button

If you still cannot depress the shutter, don't force it, as you may damage the camera. Remove the film and take the camera to be repaired.

Camera and lens care

An SLR camera is a precision-made instrument. Take care to protect it from heat, dust, sand and water. When you have finished using your camera, get into the habit of putting it away in its ever-ready case (p.89) to cushion it against knocks. Never leave your equipment in a hot place, such as the glove pocket or back shelf of an automobile. Beware of water and fine sand at the beach; keep your equipment in a waterproof bag. If you do get water or sand in the camera, have it cleaned by an

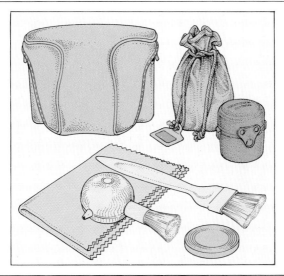

expert. Remove the batteries when storing the camera for a long time, to prevent possible leakage. You should protect your lenses from scratches, fingermarks, moisture, dust and intense sunlight. Always keep lens caps on both ends of any lenses you are not using, and store them in their protective cases. If you want to clean a lens, remove dust first with a camel hair brush or, better still, a puffer brush. Then wipe over the lens gently with an antistatic camera lens cloth. *Never* breathe on the lens and wipe it with a handkerchief.

Selecting viewpoint

There are endless ways of photographing a subject, inside or out of doors, so before you shoot, move around and examine it from different angles and heights. Notice how the image in your frame is affected. The background changes, and altered perspective influences the subject's shape. Whichever viewpoint you decide on, always make sure that your subject fills the frame. The most obvious viewpoint of our subject, right, was from the side, at normal height. The result is acceptable – a straightforward record; but it looks unimaginative and posed. An oblique view, below, places more emphasis on the horse, but the overall effect is similar.

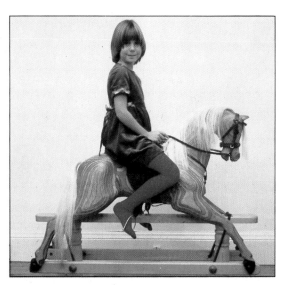

Front view
A head-on view at normal height makes both horse and child look flat, two-dimensional and uninteresting.

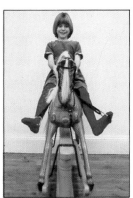

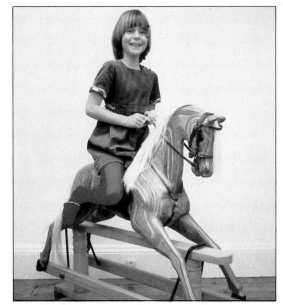

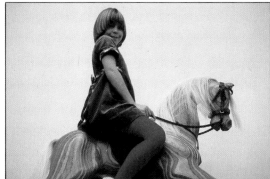

Low down and high up
A low viewpoint, shot from a kneeling position, makes the child look tall against the plain wall. By contrast, a high viewpoint, taken standing on a chair, diminishes the subject and makes the horse merge with the wooden floor.

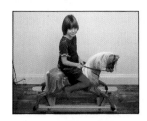

Using your imagination

A good choice of viewpoint will help you to achieve a pleasing result, but you must be imaginative if you want to create more memorable pictures. The photographer took the delightful shot, right, from the horse's tail and asked the child to turn around. A low viewpoint, close in, far right, makes the horse appear larger and more powerful in relation to the child – the shot has a lively quality the others lack.

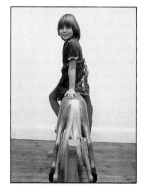

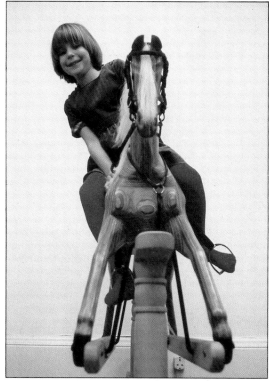

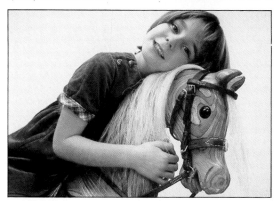

Close-ups

You will sometimes find it hard to get an uncluttered background, even after you have moved around your subject and examined it from different angles. Instead of attempting to show the whole subject, try moving right in close and concentrating on one part only, as above. This will exclude distracting background elements. Alternatively, change to a telephoto lens, in order to fill the frame from farther away and put background distractions out of focus (p.23). A longer focus lens will also avoid distortions of scale in a near subject (p.46).

Some common faults

When composing your pictures, make sure that they are not spoiled by one of the following:

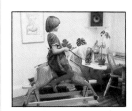

- You may want to include other objects to provide a context for your subject. Be careful how you arrange them. It is usually better to keep the background as clear as possible.

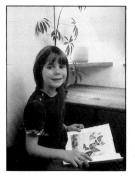

- A plant may make an attractive addition to the shot, but it shouldn't look as though it is growing straight out of the subject's head.

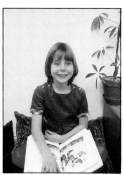

- Watch your framing. Look all around the viewfinder and make sure that your shot is not being spoiled by distracting objects coming in to the edges of the frame.

Composition and depth

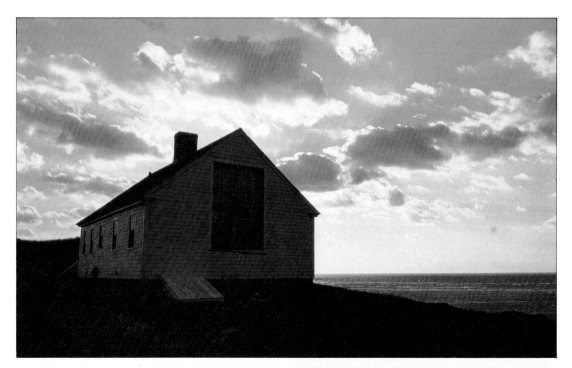

Careful framing can create a striking, well-composed picture from a simple scene, like the one above. The off-center position of the house is strong and dynamic, while the low horizon emphasizes the dramatic sky. The picture uses the "rule of thirds", shown right. Imagine lines dividing your frame into thirds. Position your main subject at one of the four intersections and let the lines suggest divisions of the frame. A centered subject often looks static, while a central horizon tends to split a picture into halves of equal size.

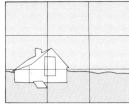

Balance
A shot composed of objects of the same color, size or shape may look repetitive and dull. You will create a livelier effect by balancing dissimilar objects. The shot right balances horizontal against vertical, bright color against neutral tone.

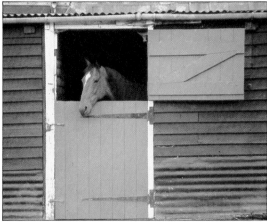

Line to emphasize mood

Many subjects have a predominance of one kind of line – horizontal, vertical or diagonal. Each of these conveys a special mood, which you can exploit by careful framing. Horizontal lines, below, convey balance and calm. Vertical lines suggest height and grandeur, as in the telephoto shot right. Diagonal lines, far right, are restless and dynamic. Let the dominant lines of your subject dictate whether you choose to frame the picture horizontally or vertically.

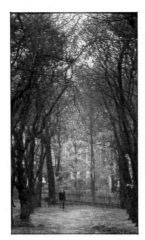

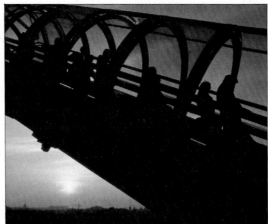

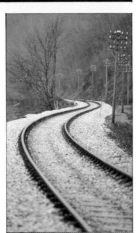

Using the foreground

If you leave the foreground empty, your shot is likely to be flat and dull. Don't waste space – use the foreground to create depth or emphasis in your pictures (p.69). A foreground frame will draw the eye into the picture and focus attention on the main subject. Try shooting through an arch or window, left, or improvise by using low-hanging foliage to frame your shot. Take care to read exposure for the main subject area (p. 19) of the picture.

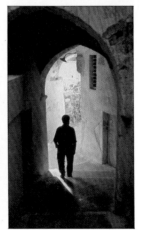

Line to suggest depth

You can also use line to suggest depth if you choose the right viewpoint. In the picture right, the curve of the railway line links the foreground to the background, leading the eye into the scene. An oblique viewpoint has exaggerated the curve, adding rhythm to the picture. The parallel lines of the pier, far right, appear to converge as they recede. The perspective effect is strengthened by the low camera viewpoint. A high viewpoint would have foreshortened the pier and reduced the sense of depth.

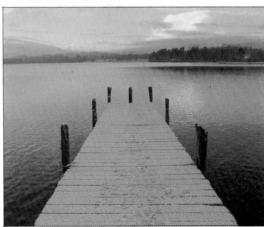

Portraying action

Good photographs of moving subjects depend on careful planning. Viewpoint, timing, focus, choice of lens, and shutter speed all play a part – whether you want to freeze action, or use blur to suggest movement.

Frozen action appears most dramatic if the subject is caught in mid-movement, as right. You can freeze action with flash (p.82) if it is in range, but otherwise you will have to rely on shutter speed (see chart facing). You can use slower shutter speeds for action moving head on to the camera, or away from it, or at a distance. Action moving across the frame, or close up, requires much faster shutter speeds. A telephoto lens enlarges and isolates action, but you must use higher speeds. The shot, right, was taken on a 200 mm "mirror" telephoto.

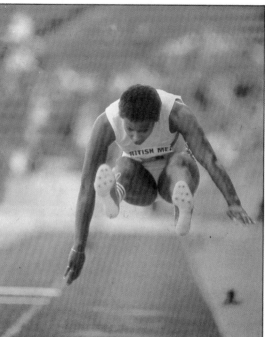

Shutter speeds for action
The chart below shows the minimum shutter speeds required to freeze various kinds of motion. Subjects traveling across your path (↔) require faster speeds than those traveling directly toward or away (↕). When shooting closer than the distances given, or with a telephoto lens, increase shutter speed.

Types of motion
Walking, talking and moving hands; slow rivers; trees in light wind.

	↔	↕
7–9 ft	1/250 sec	1/125 sec
10–15 ft	1/125 sec	1/60 sec

Running; children playing; swimmers; horse trotting; waves breaking.

	↔	↕
7–9 ft	1/500 sec	1/250 sec
10–15 ft	1/250 sec	1/125 sec

Vehicle or cycle at 30 m.p.h.; horse racing; skiers; motorboats.

	↔	↕
10–15 ft	1/1000 sec	1/500 sec
30 ft	1/500 sec	1/250 sec
60 ft	1/250 sec	1/125 sec

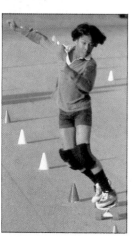

Peak action and prefocus
Action often slows, or halts at its peak – the top of a leap, for instance, or the height of a skateboarder's run, as right. Such moments make dramatic shots, and are easier to freeze. A subject moving head on shows expression clearly and is also easier to freeze, left. Plan your viewpoint so that the action will be set against a clean background. Then preset your focus on the point where the action will enter the frame, choosing something to guide you like one of the marker cones as in the picture, left.

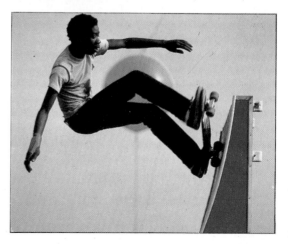

Panning and zooming

You can stop action moving across the camera by "panning" – following it with your camera as you press the shutter. With very fast subjects, right, the effect is dramatic. The background is reduced to streaks of color and part of the subject is pin sharp, part blurred. With slower movement, below, you should get the whole subject sharp. A zoom lens, far right, creates rays of soft color from a sharp subject. For all these shots, try shutter speeds of 1/8 or 1/15 sec, and prefocus. It helps to use a tripod.

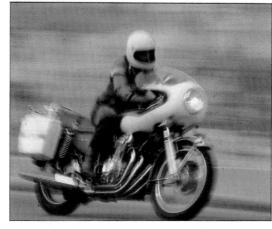

Zoom with action

You will get more sense of movement with slow action if you use a zoom lens. Try a shutter speed of 1/8 sec, and prefocus with the lens at maximum focal length. Zoom back as you pan slightly to hold the subject in the frame.

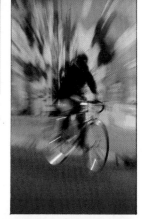

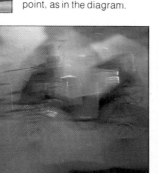

How to pan

Set your shutter to l/15 sec, and prefocus on a spot the subject will pass. Swing the camera back, and when you see the subject, pan smoothly to keep it in the frame, pressing the shutter as it passes the prefocused point, as in the diagram.

Blur/camera movement

At slow shutter speeds, moving figures blur, colors soften, and camera shake is apparent. Results can be atmospheric, as in the shot of a city square, above. Smooth, planned camera movement, on a tripod, will turn lights into patterns.

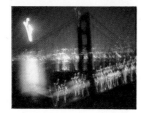

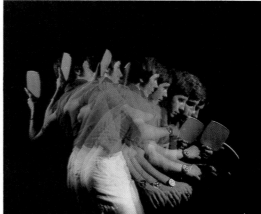

Multiple images

Multiple images are very effective to show the nature of some types of movement, as shown above. But the techniques are advanced, involving much trial and error. Here, the photographer placed flash units each side of the subject in a darkened studio, and set the camera on a tripod. Leaving the shutter open, he then fired the flash again and again, as the subject repeatedly performed the movement in slow motion. He covered the lens between flashes to keep the images sharp.

Shooting by natural light

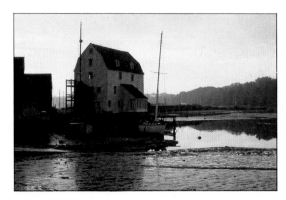 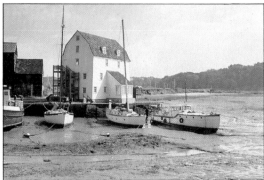

Light is perpetually changing – in color, direction and quality. And in changing, it alters the appearance of the world around us. Different subjects call for different kinds of lighting. You must learn to recognize the kind of light that will enhance the qualities and mood of your particular subject. Often it is just a question of noticing and using natural light as it occurs. Sometimes you can exploit and improve it by moving around your subject (see facing page).

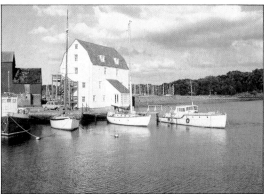

Time of day
Between sunrise and sunset, daylight presents a range of colors and moods. At dawn, top left, colors are muted and outlines softened. By mid-morning, top right, the sun is high in the sky, casting hard-edged shadows. The early afternoon sun, center, brings out strong color and detail. By late afternoon the sun is starting to set, below left, bathing the scene in a golden light, while dusk, below, creates a cool, mysterious mood.

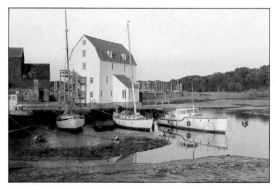 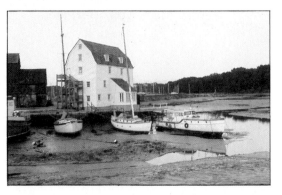

The direction of light
As the sun moves across the sky, it strikes the earth at different angles. At noon, you must be content with overhead lighting. At other times of day you can alter the angle of the lighting in your shot by moving around your subject.

Side-lighting, below left, reveals the texture and form of the tide-mill, where back-lighting, below, throws the building into dramatic silhouette, suppressing all color and detail. Front-lighting, right, flattens both form and texture but enhances color.

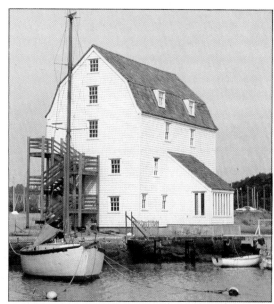

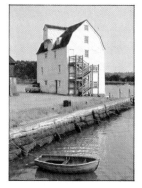

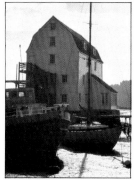

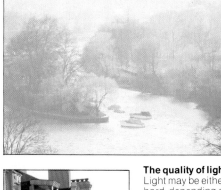

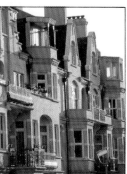

The quality of light
Light may be either soft or hard, depending on weather and time of day. When the sun is filtered by cloud, mist or rain, it gives soft, even lighting which mutes color and brings out detail, above. When the sun is bright and direct, shining from overhead or behind the camera, it gives hard, frontal lighting with sharp-edged shadows, left. Storms can produce dramatic colors and penetrating shafts of light, right.

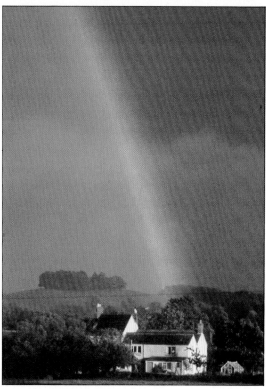

Shooting with flash

Flash provides a convenient, portable source of daylight. You can use it both indoors and out to supplement existing light, brighten colors, fill in shadows or freeze action (p.82). Its main drawback is that you cannot see in advance how it will affect your subject, nor where shadows will fall. Shining a lamp in place of the flash will allow you to predict its effect more accurately. Always keep your subjects at the same distance to avoid flash fall-off. But bear in mind that you can use fall-off deliberately to darken a cluttered background. Try using flash to brighten up a dimly lit interior, like the bar room, right.

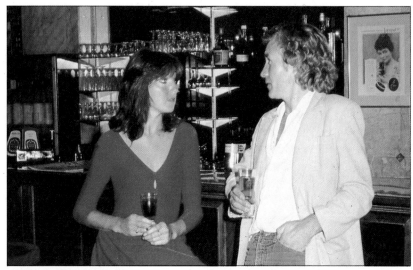

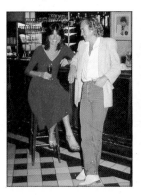

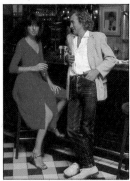

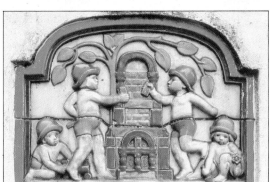

Flash or available light?
Flash has enriched colors and illuminated background detail in the picture above. But the girl has a lifeless, glazed expression. You will create a more natural effect (and avoid the possibility of "red eye") if you ask people not

to look directly at the flash gun, as in the top shot. Shooting by available light, above, has recorded more of the atmosphere of the bar. But colors are duller and shadow detail is lost. Using room lights with daylight slide film has given a warm cast (p.17).

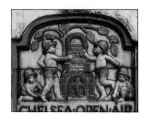

Flash for bright color
Toward the end of the day or when the sky is overcast, there is not enough light to do justice to the colors and details of a small object, like the plaque, left. So use flash to simulate sunlight and brighten colors, as in the picture above.

Creating softer lighting

Flash is a fairly hard, directional light source that can cast ugly shadows. You can create softer, more even lighting by diffusing it. Cover the flash head with one layer of white

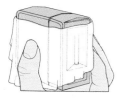

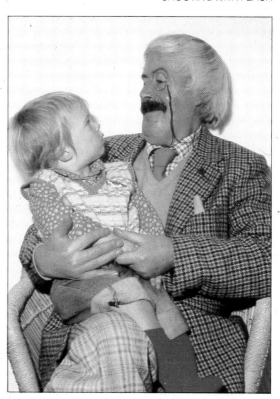

handkerchief, as above, or use a ready-made diffuser. Or try bouncing the flash, as below, off a white wall or ceiling, if you can tilt it or use it off camera. Open up the lens two stops.

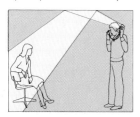

Flash portraits

For portraiture, direct on-camera flash is too harsh. Like the midday sun, it tends to flatten features and throw sharp-edged shadows, as shown above. If you can take your flash-gun off camera, you can use it to side-light or back-light your subject. Alternatively, try bouncing or diffusing it, as described left. In the picture right, diffused flash has minimized the shadows behind the figures and revealed shadow detail.

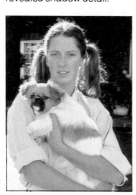

Using flash fill-in

Dark shadows are often a problem when you take portraits in bright sunlight or by a window. For a less contrasty result, you can use your flash to lighten or "fill in" areas of densest shadow. When using flash as fill-in you should reduce

its effect (p.21) so that it does not dominate the natural light. Back-lighting has obscured the face with shadow while rimming the head with a halo of light, above left. Fill-in flash shows more detail in the face but retains the halo effect, above.

Flash faults

"Red-eye" is seen in close-ups of people and animals when on-camera flash has been used at subject eye-level. It is most pronounced when available light is very dim and the iris of the eye is wide open. Either use flash off camera, directed at your subject from an angle. Or increase room lighting and leave flash on camera, but diffused. On-camera flash may also produce intrusive flare spots if you shoot facing a mirror, window or other reflective surface. Placing the flash at an oblique angle is the best way to avoid reflections.

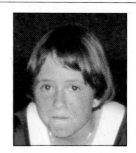

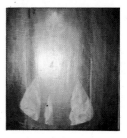

Expressive black and white

Black and white is graphic or abstract, where color is sensual and realistic. Use it to bring out texture, to simplify lines and shapes, or to provide atmosphere.

The main advantage of black and white is its simplicity. A subject that is overwhelmed by a mass of colors will look much more powerful when reproduced in black and white. Try using its subtle range of tones to suggest texture, right. Indirect light or side-lighting will enhance the textural effect (p.33). Or choose it when you want to emphasize a strong shape. Frame your subject against a background of contrasting tone for additional impact, as below. A sharp black/white contrast of highlights and dense shadows makes a strikingly dramatic picture, below right.

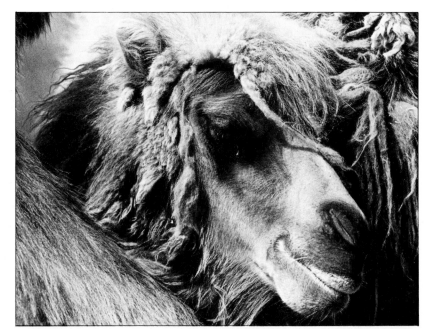

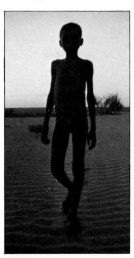

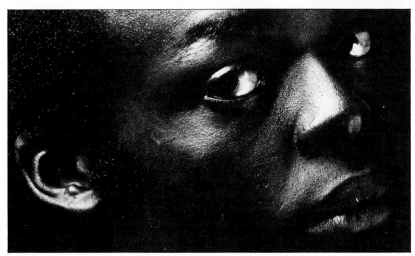

Coping with dim light

Black and white film is the best choice for a dusk shot or a dimly lit interior, such as the bar room, right. It is available in higher speeds than color film, enabling you to freeze movement even in dull conditions. And the grainy quality of the film adds atmosphere. If color had been used for the picture right, the cluttered background might have distracted attention from the people. And, on color slide film, the mixed lighting would have caused a color cast (p.17).

● If the film in your camera is too slow for prevailing lighting conditions, remember that you can uprate it (p.17).

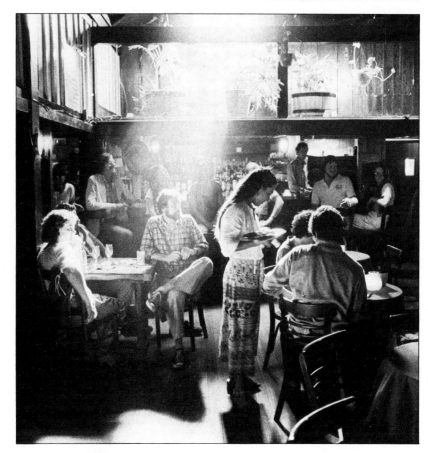

Manipulating your print

Black and white film is both easier and cheaper to manipulate in the darkroom. There are various ways in which your negatives can be printed to create a special effect. They can be sepia-toned, trimmed ("cropped") to give a stronger composition, or "vignetted" (printed in a soft, oval frame). Or ask your processor to modify the range of tones to create a predominantly dark and dramatic (low-key) or light, romantic (high-key) print.

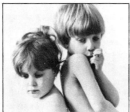

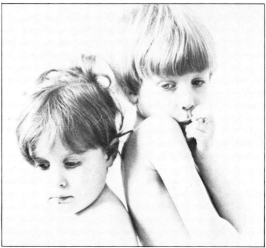

Creating a high-key mood

The soft, delicate tones of the portrait right were produced in the darkroom. The unmodified original is shown above. If you want to achieve a high-key effect, choose a basically light-toned subject and use soft, indirect lighting so as to avoid creating harsh, unflattering shadows.

Strong and muted color

Strong color is vibrant and bold. Only bright, direct lighting will bring out its full brilliance.

Color is the single most powerful element in any picture, so you should control it carefully. Generally, a restricted color range is more effective than a mass of unrelated colors. The shot of the bus, right, is bright and colorful without being gaudy – strong colors are well balanced by more neutral tones. Taking a detail from the bus picture, below, strengthens color contrast and simplifies the composition. You will achieve the most dynamic color contrast if you offset warm colors with cold ones – reds and yellows against blues and greens.

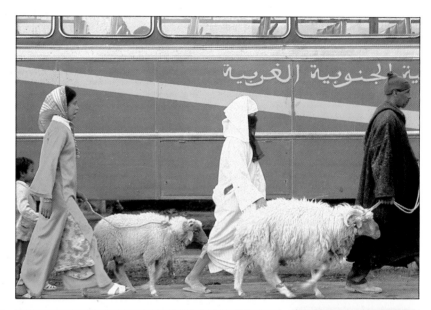

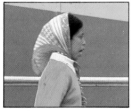

Finding isolated color
Even a relatively small area of strong color will dominate a picture when set against a neutral or monochromatic background, right. When the sky is overcast and dull, the sea gray and stormy, or the scene drab, look out for chance occurrences of isolated color.

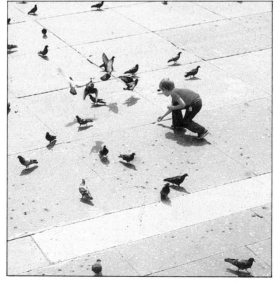

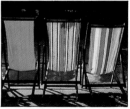

Color for color's sake
Moving in close to the striped canvas chairs, above, has created a bold, semi-abstract picture, using color for color's sake. The effect is enriched by back-lighting. Multiple color contrast requires careful handling – keep the composition as simple as possible, and frame your subject tightly in order to exclude completely any weaker color elements.

Muted color can be romantic, bleak or dramatic. Soft lighting brings out its subtle range of tones.

In the shaded street scene, right, diffused lighting has softened and merged colors and shapes. Even the bright blue stripes of the towel appear subdued. Look for muted colors when light is scattered by haze, rain or smoke.

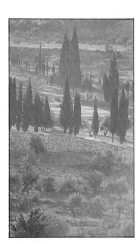

Harmony in nature
You can convey a feeling of harmony by restricting your view to a range of tones of one particular color, as above, or a variety of pastel shades. Nature provides an ideal source of inspiration for harmonious color pictures. In the landscape above, the repetition of the shapes of the trees adds greatly to the tranquil mood and the harmony of the composition.

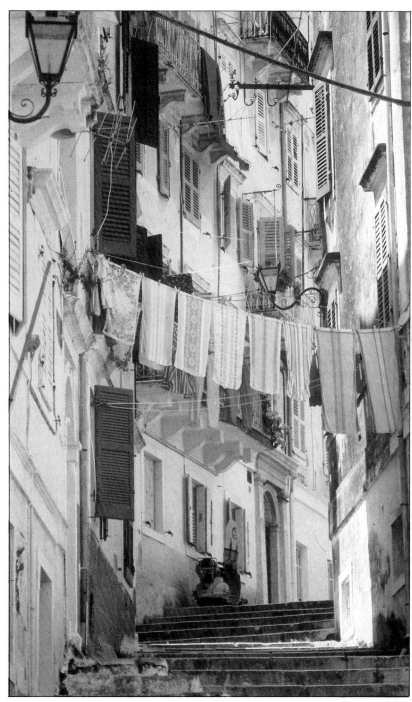

Shooting at night

There is a great variety of challenging subjects for night shots, whether you hand-hold the camera and use 400 ASA film or take advantage of the SLR's facility for long exposures.

The pictures on this page were all taken with the camera hand-held (see chart on facing page). To allow an exposure brief enough for you to hold the camera steady, use a 50 mm lens, as this usually has the widest maximum aperture. And concentrate on subjects that are well lit. Try shooting at dusk, when there is enough light to record some detail and the sky looks like night, as right.

● Remember that you can increase your film speed by uprating the film (p. 17).

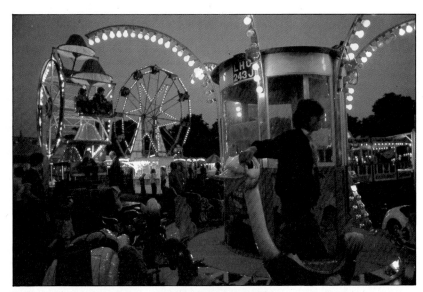

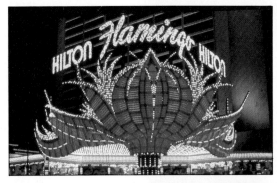

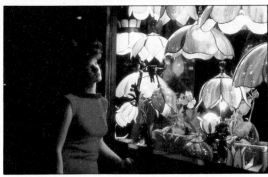

Shooting light sources
Try shooting light sources for their own sake. A large neon sign fills the frame with sharp pinpoints of light, above. Defocusing (p.11) blurs street lights into discs, right, creating an effective, abstract pattern of different colors.

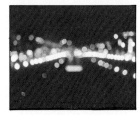

Brightly lit areas
Take advantage of brightly lit areas if you want to avoid using a long exposure. Shopping centers, store windows and cinema or theater entrances provide a bright, even spill of light. To photograph a person at night, stand your subject close to the light source, so that the face is well lit, as above. Shooting after rain when sidewalks are wet and reflective will help to light up a dark foreground. Tungsten slide film gives more accurate coloring than daylight slide film for tungsten-lit street scenes.

Using a long exposure

A far wider range of night shots is available to you if you use a long exposure (over 1/30 sec) and set the camera on a tripod. If you require exposure over 1 sec, use the "B" setting (p.13) to take a time exposure and trigger the shutter with a cable release (p.15).

Gaining depth of field

When you want to record detail over a large area at night, use a long exposure and stop down the lens to maximize depth of field. In the river scene, right, shot at 1/4 sec at f11, both the tiny ripples in the foreground and the buildings in the distance are sharply defined.
● Read exposure carefully at night. Bracket your shots to be sure of a good result.

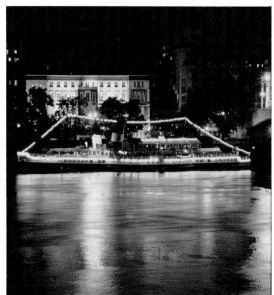

Exposure times

This chart shows the shutter speeds suggested with 400 ASA color film for a variety of subjects. It assumes a wide aperture (f2.8) except for the starred items (f16).

Dusk shots	1/60 sec
Store windows	1/60 sec
Theater entrances	1/60 sec
Neon signs	1/60 sec
Well-lit street	1/30 sec
Portrait by bonfire	1/30 sec
Street lights	1/15 sec
City panorama	1/15 sec
Campfires	1/15 sec
Floodlit buildings	1/8 sec
Candlelight	1/4 sec
Auto light trails ⁕	1/2 sec
Fireworks ⁕	1 sec
Full moon landscape	10–30 secs
Moon and star trails ⁕	20 mins

Light trails

During a 5 sec exposure, moving automobile lights trace luminous streaks of light across the frame.

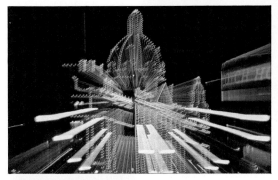

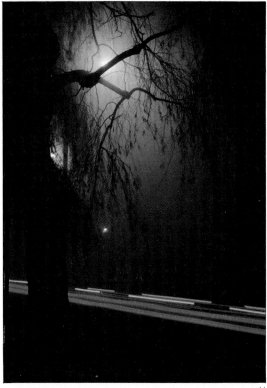

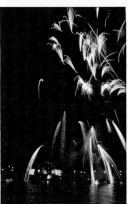

Zooming

A zoom lens has transformed the lights into radiating bars, above. Focus with the lens at longest focal length. Then using a long exposure (1/2 or 1 sec) fire the shutter as you zoom back.

Fireworks

When shooting a firework display, stop down and use a time exposure to keep the shutter open for several bursts. Cover the lens between bursts, so that you don't overexpose the rest of your image.

Candids–the unobserved camera

The appeal of candid shots lies in their naturalness and spontaneity. To achieve this, your subject should be oblivious of the camera. This means shooting either when people are engrossed in an activity or when you can remain unobserved by using an unexpected viewpoint or by shooting from farther away with a 135 or 200 mm lens. The expressions and emotions that make a strong candid shot are fleeting so you must work quickly. Preset focus and work out depth of field in advance (p.13). And take light readings from the back of your hand to gauge exposure for your subject's face (p.19). A prompt response to the moment captured the delight of the woman, right, watching street theater.

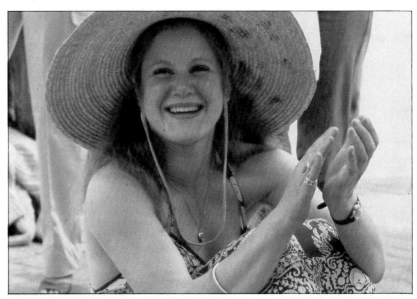

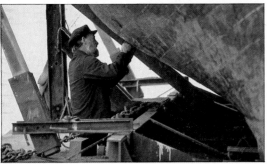

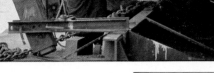

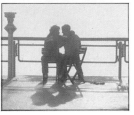

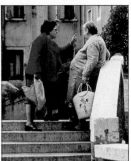

Different viewpoints
You can often get closer to your subject without being seen by choosing an unusual viewpoint. A low side view provided an informal shot of a man at work on his boat, above. A rear view caught the couple, right, unawares.

Using a long focus lens
A telephoto lens enabled the photographer to pick this little girl out from a crowd of spectators, while still keeping his distance. Its limited depth of field blurred shapes and colors in the background, giving a soft contrasting frame.

People in conversation
Look out for interesting gestures and expressions when people are talking. The picture above captured the precise moment when the women's postures and gestures were most telling. A 135 mm lens picked out the expressive face, right.

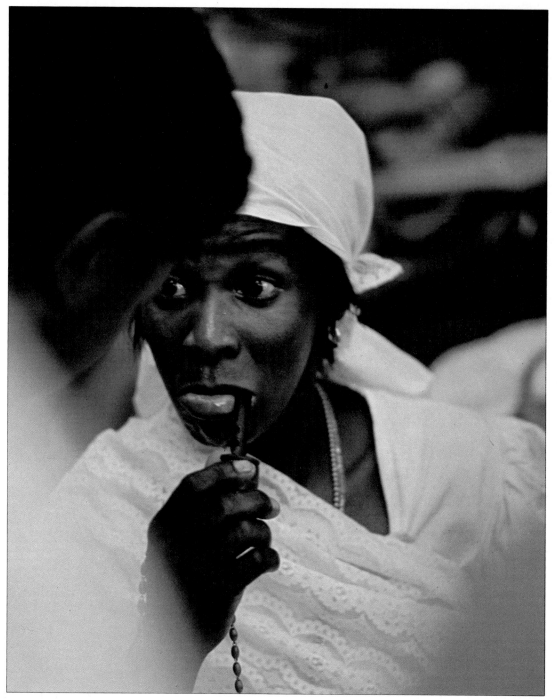

Informal family pictures

The pictures you take of your family at home are likely to be among your most successful. You are working with people that you know well and your equipment is always at hand when an exciting picture-taking opportunity arises. Don't allow familiarity with your home to blind you to distracting background details and colors. Watch out for highly patterned wallpaper and furnishings in the house, and bright flowers and shrubs outside. Whenever possible, shoot by natural light indoors, using a slow shutter speed or fast film, and choose soft, diffused sunlight outside. For an informal group shot, right, pose the family around a center of interest (p.70).

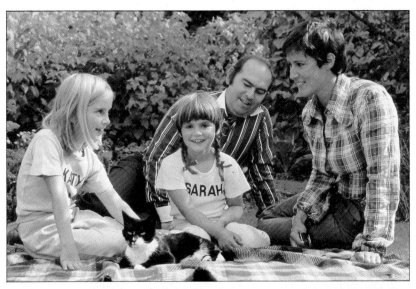

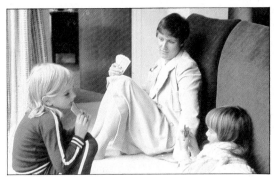

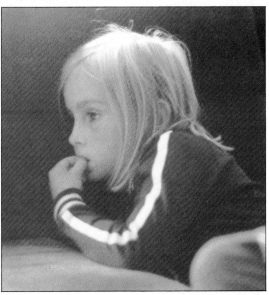

Choosing the moment
Timing is as important as any technical skill when taking pictures of people. Wait until faces and gestures are animated, as above, then shoot quickly. Don't economize on film – it may take several shots to get a lively composition.

Capturing expressions
A child's quieter moments can be just as revealing as her livelier moods, as right. Move in close to catch characteristic expressions, or better still, change to a telephoto lens and keep your distance, so that she is undisturbed (p.42).

Double portraits

When photographing two people, try to express the relationship between them. Shoot when they are looking at each other, as below, or in the same direction, far right. The picture will lack unity if they are looking in opposite directions, right.

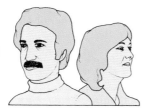

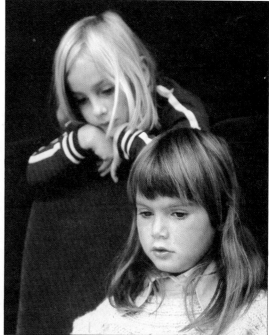

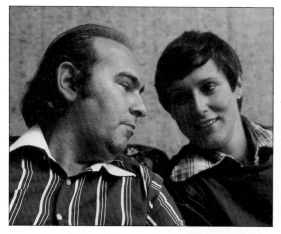

Shooting unobserved

You will achieve the most natural, unselfconscious pictures of your family when they are unaware of the camera. Shoot while they are absorbed in an activity, selecting a viewpoint that shows clearly what they are doing, as right. Here, low back-lighting from the window has muted colors and provided a soft frame for the children. Even in such dim lighting, don't be tempted to use flash. Besides drawing attention to the camera, flash tends to destroy atmosphere. Provided subject movement is minimal, you can still shoot by natural light if you use a wide aperture combined with a slow shutter speed. Or, if you want to increase depth of field, stop down and use an even slower shutter, with the camera firmly supported, or change to a faster film.

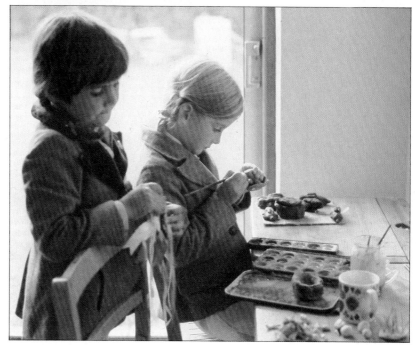

Portrait techniques

Taking good portraits is not always easy, but a combination of time, care and patience will give you excellent results. Choose a fairly close viewpoint, say 4–5 ft (1.2–1.5 m), so that your subject dominates the frame (p.27). Then study him from different sides. Few people have such regular features that they look equally good from all angles. A three-quarter view, right, generally seems the most natural. Whenever possible, choose a plain background, taking into account coloring and clothing. If surroundings are cluttered, check depth of field (p.13) to see whether they will be in focus. Never allow the background to dominate, as far right. Instead, either move your subject away or open up the lens to a wider aperture and put it out of focus. Read exposure directly from your sitter's face and focus on the eyes.

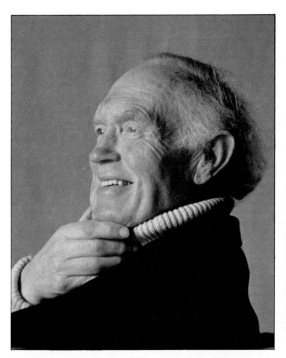

Relaxing your subject
Success in portrait-taking depends largely on your ability to relax your subject. Keep him talking while you shoot or wait until he is absorbed in an activity. Never ask him to stand still and look into the lens, as below.

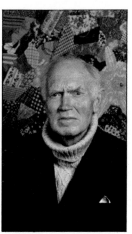

Which lens is best?
Take care when choosing a lens for close-up portraits. A 28 mm lens, near right, magnifies features nearest the camera and distorts the face. A standard lens, center, still causes perceptible distortion when the face fills the frame. The ideal choice is the 135 mm telephoto lens, far right. This records facial proportions accurately and enables you to use a more distant viewpoint.

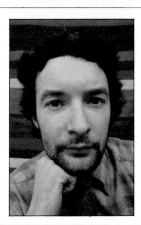
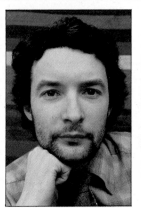
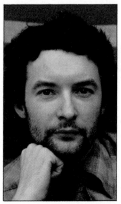

Using light outdoors
Strong overhead sunlight can make people squint and may cast shadows beneath the eyes, nose and chin, below left. You can usually create a more flattering effect by turning your sitter's head until the face is in light shadow and the sun highlights the hair, below right. Hazy or cloudy days, right, provide the best lighting conditions. The soft, diffused light produces good facial modeling and your subject can look comfortably at the camera, no matter how high the sun is in the sky.

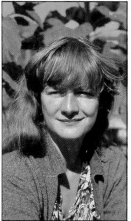 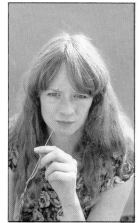 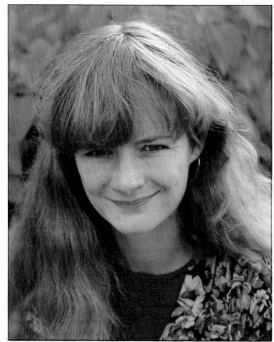

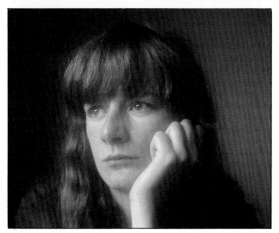 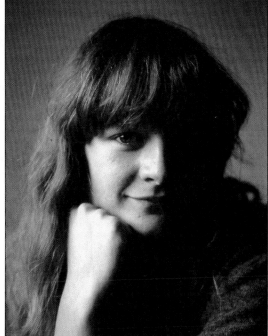

Using light indoors
When taking indoor portraits, use fast film and position your sitter about 4 ft (1.2 m) from a window. On a sunny day, the light may be harsh and directional. To soften the lighting and create a more romantic effect, smear a little grease on a plain filter and use this in front of the lens while you shoot, as above. Or exploit dramatic lighting contrast by taking your sitter side-on to the window, as right. Read exposure from the lit side of your subject's face.

Babies–the first year

Owning a camera gives you the unique opportunity to make a visual diary of your baby's progress. During his first year, a baby masters many new skills – from feeding himself to crawling and walking – so take pictures regularly. When shooting indoors, try to use natural lighting; outside, soft, even light is best. The extra magnification of a telephoto lens is useful for a head shot, but when lighting is dim, you will require the wider maximum aperture of a standard lens (p.22). Don't pose your baby or dress him specially. Get down to his level and take him among his toys in familiar surroundings. A very young baby will feel most secure when cradled in his mother's arms, right.

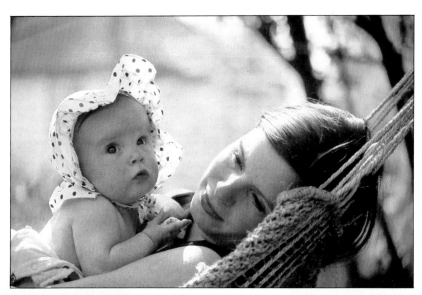

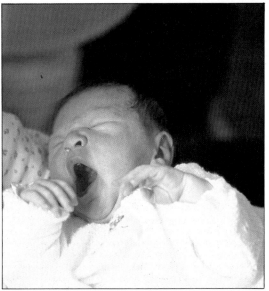

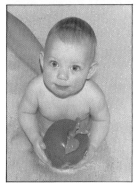

Propping your baby up
Until a baby can sit up on his own, you will have to find some way of supporting him. Try propping him up on soft-toned cushions or pillows. Or let his head rest against someone's arm. If possible, choose a viewpoint that hides the supporting arm behind the baby – in the picture right it is intrusive and diverts attention from the subject.

Expressive moments
Babies make delightfully unselfconscious subjects for photography. But their emotions and expressions change rapidly. So have your camera ready at all times and be prepared to work fast. A quick reaction to the moment was required to capture the baby just as he was yawning, left.

Focusing close-ups
When a baby is old enough to move around on her own, as right, it becomes harder to keep close-ups in focus. Rather than continually adjusting the focusing ring, lean back and forth after rough focusing and shoot when the image looks sharp.

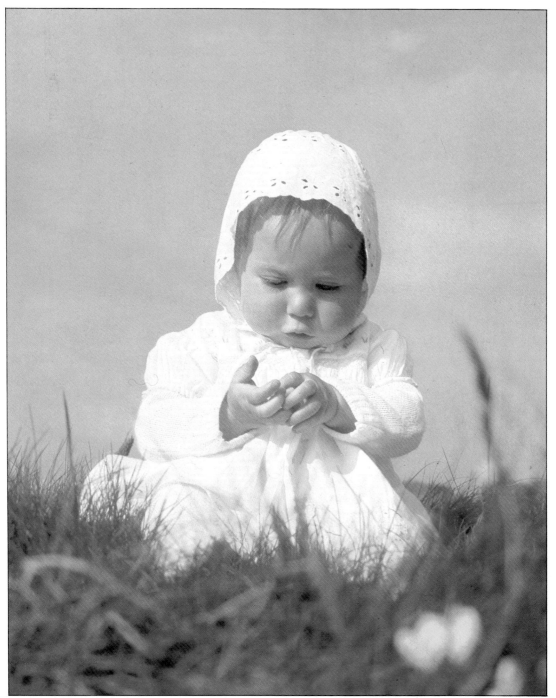

Children–the natural subject

Children can be lively and excited one moment, quiet and pensive the next. Make the most of their ever-changing moods and expressions by taking your camera with you on all occasions. Use a tele-photo lens so that you can shoot from a distance without intruding.

Ready-made situations
You will capture children at their most spontaneous when their attention is absorbed. A trip to the fair, below, provided a tailor-made chance for a candid shot. The photographer preset focus and exposure.

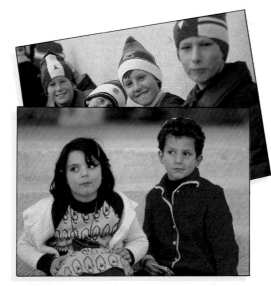

Common errors
Both the pictures left are ruined by self-consciousness. The boys are acting up to the camera while the pair below are already bored by being photographed. You can avoid results like this by giving children something absorbing to do.

Unusual viewpoints
An unusual viewpoint often helps you take pictures without being seen – giving you time to consider composition. In the shot below notice how the girl's leg and boy's arm create a pleasing sense of balance.

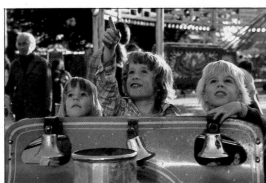

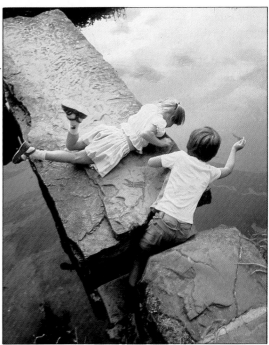

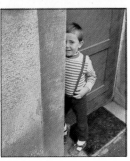

Coping with a shy child
If a child is shy of the camera, you can often put him at ease by turning the whole occasion into a game. Try letting him take your picture instead, or join in a game of peek-a-boo, as in the picture left.

Using light and color

You can greatly enhance the mood of your shots by using color and lighting sensitively. Back-lighting adds a bright, sunny mood to the picture of the little girl below, caught in a high-spirited moment. Exposure was read for her face (p.19). Dull lighting and a somber background tone echo the pensive mood of the boy, below right. The brilliant yellow balloon provides a strident contrast with clothing and background colors. The dreamy, slightly wistful mood of the little boy at the window, right, is enhanced by soft lighting and harmonious tones.

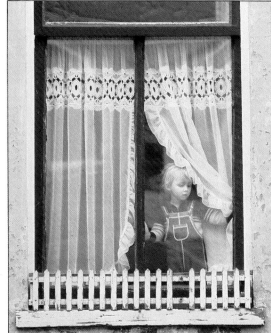

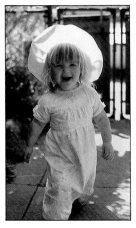

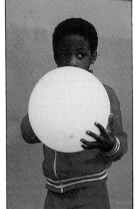

Capturing children at play

The seashore provides children with an endless source of fascination. Absorbed in play, they will soon forget the camera, enabling you to shoot freely. Be patient and wait until an interesting situation develops. Then shoot fast, before the moment is gone, as right. The diagram below shows what happens if your reactions are too slow.

● Always take children from their own level – a normal, standing viewpoint will give a distorted impression.

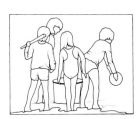

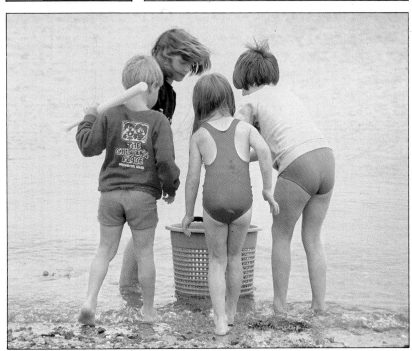

Weddings and receptions

Weddings are unrepeatable events, so make sure your camera is working properly and take plenty of film. Don't attempt to cover all aspects of a wedding – concentrate on capturing the mood of the occasion, and leave the traditional poses to the professional. If you try to tackle the more formal shots, you may well get pictures like those right. The group shot is badly organized and mistimed. In the church shot, flash has created a harsh light and dazzled the groom. If possible, try to use available light to advantage, below right.

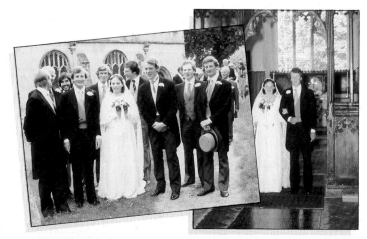

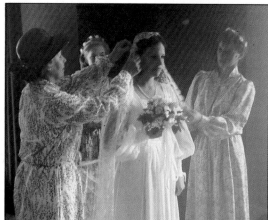

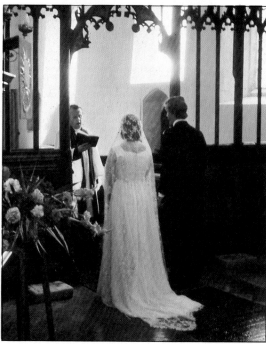

Final preparations
Sunlight streaming through a window has sidelit the group above, delicately modeling their faces. The photographer breathed on a clear filter fixed over the lens in order to soften contrast and enhance the romantic effect (p.88).

Inside the church
If you want to record the ceremony, ask permission first and find a suitable camera position before the service. For the picture right, viewpoint was chosen to include both priest and flowers. Lighting will be dim so use fast film and a tripod.

Using a wide-angle
Exploit the broad field of view of a wide-angle lens to encompass scenes like the wedding feast. Or use its qualities of distortion – here a 28 mm lens has exaggerated the elegant lines of the wedding car.

Seizing the moment
Don't miss an opportunity to shoot the bridal pair unobserved; as when the official photographer is arranging them, below.

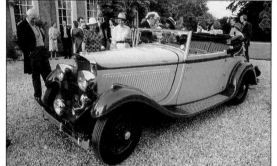

The wedding guests
Move around after the ceremony and take some candid pictures of the wedding guests. Most will be too busy enjoying themselves to pay any attention to you. The photographer captured the pair, below left, with a shutter speed of 1/125 sec, as they ran toward the camera. A low viewpoint was used to take this shot of the little boy with his mother, below.

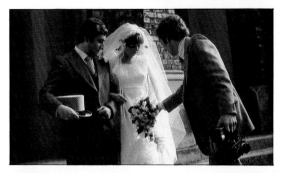

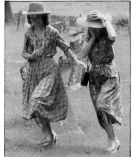

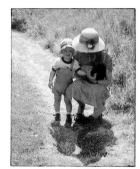

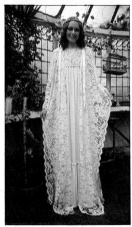

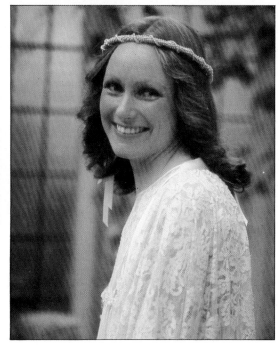

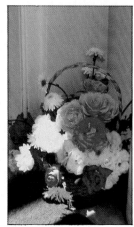

Bridal portraits
Step back for a full-length portrait of the bride in her wedding gown, as above. Stop down to get an attractive setting, like this conservatory, in focus. But use a wide aperture and a 135 mm lens to soften an intrusive background, right.

Decorative details
Don't forget to record memorable details, like the basket of flowers, above. Move in close and frame tightly to exclude extraneous elements from the composition. When shooting at close range, be sure to focus accurately.

Pets and small creatures

Pets, like children, are challenging subjects. For good results, you require patience, quick reflexes, and an understanding of your pet's personality. Use your ingenuity to attract and hold your pet's attention, as animals soon lose interest – a strange noise will make a dog prick up his ears, a bowl of food will keep him occupied. Try taking a close-up portrait, as right. If possible, use natural light and always choose a viewpoint that catches the highlights in the animal's eyes. Avoid taking close-ups with a wide-angle lens. The steep perspective will give ugly distortions.

Anticipating the action
If your dog is bounding along, below, anticipate his path and preset focus and exposure. A fast shutter speed (1/250 or 1/500 sec) will freeze his movement as he runs past.

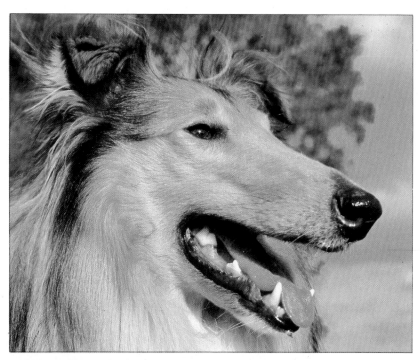

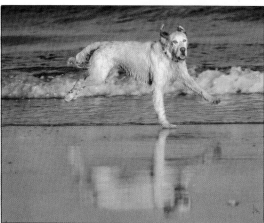

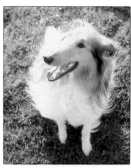

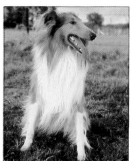

Selecting viewpoint
Photographing a pet from above foreshortens the body and makes the head appear disproportionately large, above left. Get down to the animal's own level by kneeling or lying on the ground, to capture its true proportions, as above.

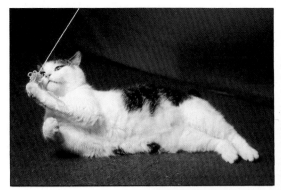
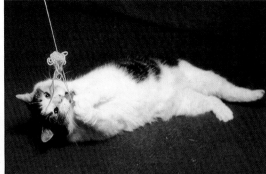

Play sequence
You will capture the greatest range of poses and expressions if you take your pet playing. Shoot a sequence in quick succession. Try to keep the same viewpoint throughout.

Small pets
Hamsters, mice, and other small pets tend to dart out of range unless securely held, as below.

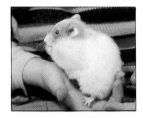

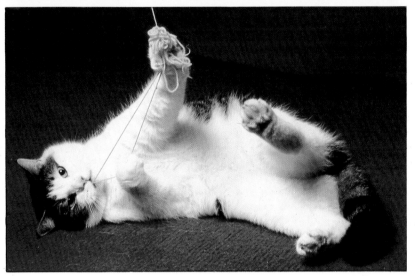

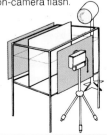

Shooting aquarium life
Set your camera on a tripod, with the lens against the glass front. To eliminate reflections, fix a piece of black card in front of the camera, with a hole for the lens. A second piece of card on the back of the tank provides a plain background. Insert a glass partition in the tank, to confine the fish and aid focusing. To light the tank, you can either use a spotlight, as in the diagram, or off-camera flash, held above the water. Flash will freeze motion, bring out color, and isolate the fish from the background, as in the picture right. Never use on-camera flash.

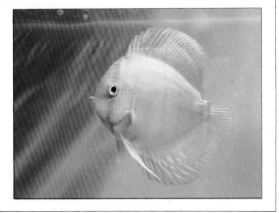

Flowers and insects close up

When shooting plants and insects, you will want to move right up close. Your standard lens, used at its minimum focusing distance, gives a reasonably satisfying result, as below right, provided your subject is not too small. But to make the most of the intricate patterning, rich colors, and textures of the natural world, it is worth buying some form of close-up attachment that allows you to shoot even nearer. A 20 mm extension tube, used only four inches away, has produced a near-life-size image of the heart of the flower, above right, bringing out its bright, contrasting colors. When working close-up, be sure to focus accurately, as depth of field is very limited. And use fairly bright lighting (or flash, diffused) so that you can stop down.

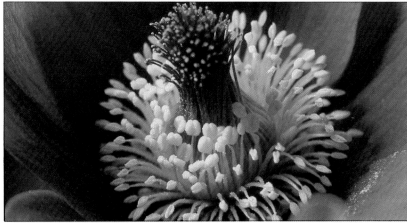

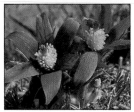

Close-ups and movement
Both camera and subject movement are magnified close up. Always use a tripod to support your camera. And, if there is the slightest breeze, position a shield of thick cardboard in the wind's path, as shown right.

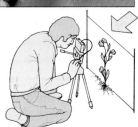

Close-up equipment
Single lens reflex cameras are ideal for close-ups – whatever attachment you use, the viewfinder still shows exactly what you will record. Most close-up attachments work by "spacing" the lens farther from the film. You either add an extension tube or concertina bellows between body and lens, or use an adaptor ring to mount the lens in reverse. The cost, advantages and disadvantages of the various types of close-up attachment or special lens are discussed in the chart, right.

Reversing ring		Cheap. Used with 50 mm lens, allows focusing down to about 5 in. But leaves protruding back end of lens vulnerable.	And difficult to use in dim light as you must view and focus at working (rather than full) aperture (p.12).
Close-up lenses		Fairly cheap. Screw on to front of lens, like filters. Made in various strengths or "diopters" and can be	combined. Allow focusing down to about 6 in. But definition falls off at picture edges.
Extension tubes		Moderate price. Best bought in sets of three different lengths, which can be used separately or combined.	Combining all three allows focusing down to about 4 in. Most types require you to focus at working aperture.
Bellows		Quite expensive. Similar to extension tubes but offer continuously variable lens extension rather than	extension in fixed steps. Allow focusing down to about 3in and can give double life-size image.
Macro lens		Expensive. Complete lens, allowing continuous focusing from infinity down to life-size image,	but designed to give best performance close up. Gives greater depth of field than any other close-up device.

Knowing your subject
Successful nature photography depends on being in the right place at the right time. You must be up early to capture the morning dew on a spider's web. Find a viewpoint that catches the light in the dewdrops and sets the web against a dark background.

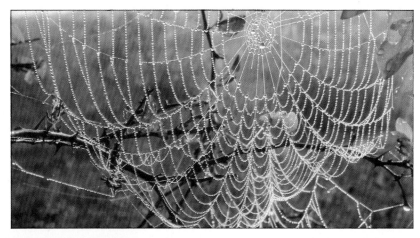

Butterflies and moths
Photographing butterflies demands a lot of time and patience. Be as quiet as you can and wait for the insect to settle, preferably on a flower or leaf of contrasting color, as below. Use flash to bring out wing color.

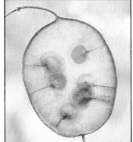

Using back-lighting
The color and shape of translucent plants show up best by strong back-lighting. In soft, diffused light the seed-pod looks dull in color and merges into the background. When backlit by strong sunlight, color is intensified and the whole pod is outlined by a halo of light.

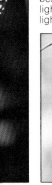

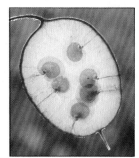

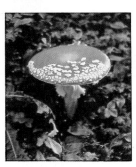

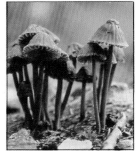

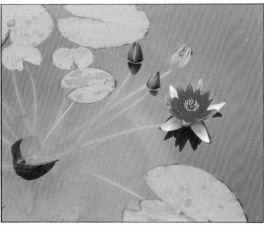

Unexpected color
Mushrooms and toadstools can be as colorful as flowers. Choose a view that reveals their best features, as shown above and right.

Framing for effect
Be imaginative in your framing, as right. Placing the lily off-center has focused attention on the bright pink flower (p.28).

Zoos and game parks

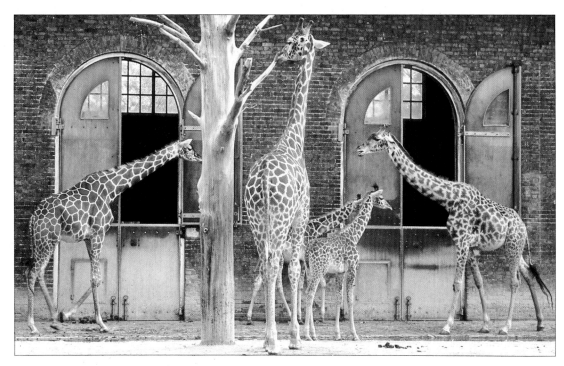

Photographing animals in zoos is not easy – they are either too far off, asleep, behind bars, or obscured by shade or ugly settings. A telephoto lens helps, but timing and viewpoint are just as important. An animal often makes regular trips around its enclosure. Observe it, and pick a spot where it will approach closely, and be in sunlight or set against a contrasting backdrop of grass, leaves or sky. Focus and set your exposure for that spot. Then wait. With large animals, try to include something that shows scale, as above.

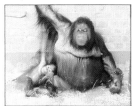

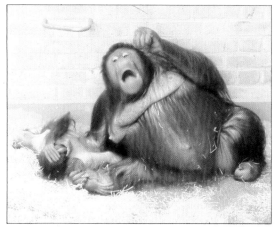

Humor and interest
A sequence of action shots in close succession from one viewpoint often conveys the humor of an animal's behavior better than one picture. This pair was busy playing up to the crowd, so the photographer had time for several shots.

Panning a moving animal
In safari parks, where animals are free to roam around, try using a strong telephoto lens and panning to freeze movement. With your camera on a tripod, use the panning head to follow the animal's movement as you release the shutter (p.31). The wildebeeste, below, was caught with legs outstretched against the blurred prairie background.

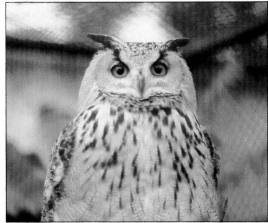

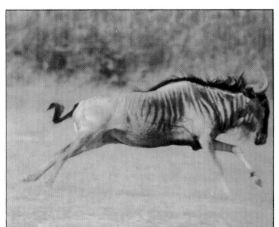

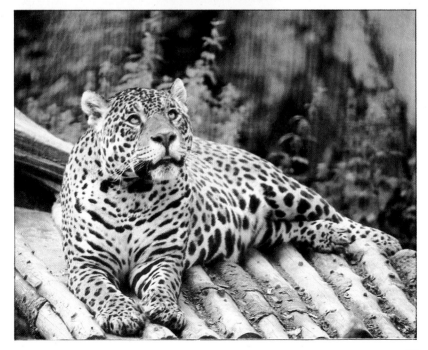

Avoiding cage bars
Zoo shots are often spoiled by intrusive bars or wire netting in the foreground, as left. To eliminate them, either position your camera so the lens "sees" between the bars. Or use a wide aperture to throw them out of focus.

Inaccessible animals
Animals in zoos are often too far away to photograph effectively with a standard lens. Take advantage of the extra magnification of a telephoto lens to make distant animals look closer. And make use of its shallow depth of field to soften distracting details in the foreground and background. In the picture right, the blurred setting serves to isolate and focus attention on the basking leopard.

Hobbies and occupations

A friend who has an interesting hobby or job makes a good subject for informal shots. Your main aim should be to link the person closely with his activity so as to show them as an integrated whole.

If you choose an intricate hobby like model-making, you will want to bring out as much color and detail as possible. This means using flash to supplement daylight, so that you can stop down and increase depth of field (p.20). Move in close to show exactly what your subject is doing. (Diffuse flash close up.) Exclude anything not closely related to the activity – a neutral background is best. Above all, try to convey the skill and concentration demanded by the hobby.

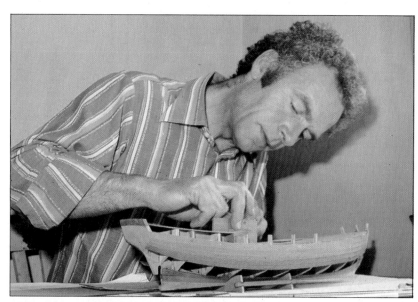

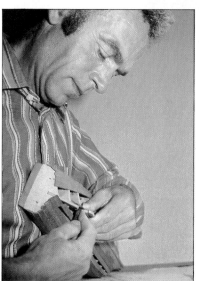

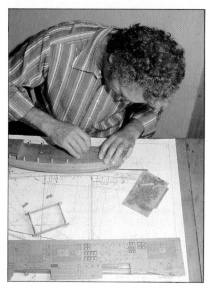

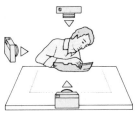

Choosing viewpoint
Before shooting, study your subject from various angles. An eye-level viewpoint, top, gives a good overall view of both man and boat. But you must get down low to show a subject's expression, as far left – people tend to lower their heads when working with their hands. Shooting from above, left, emphasizes the precise skill of the hobby. (See camera angles above.)

Capturing atmosphere

Photographing a person in his working environment demands a slightly different approach. Here it is more important to capture atmosphere than detail, so use natural light and fast film. And shoot when your subject is close to a bright light source, exposing for the face. Don't disturb your subject while he is working – your shots will be stiff and artificial if you try to stage-manage him. Look out for characteristic actions and postures that express the nature of his occupation. For the picture right the photographer stepped back to show the blacksmith framed by the tools of his trade. Grease was used on a filter to mute colors and soften the lighting (p.88).

Moving in close

A close viewpoint and low camera angle have caught the blacksmith's jovial personality, below. A tightly framed close-up focuses attention on one of his tools, bottom. A wide aperture was used to throw the background out of focus.

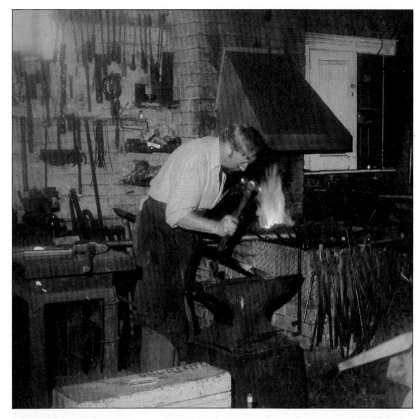

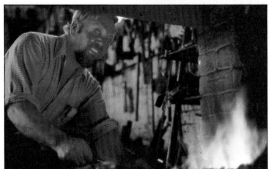

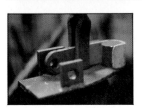

Freezing movement

400 ASA film will allow you to freeze some motion without flash, even in low lighting conditions, giving a realistic flavor to your pictures. The angle of the sparks adds dynamism to the shot right (p.29).

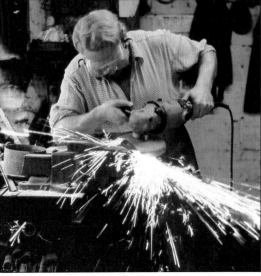

Possessions and still life

When photographing a treasured possession, take your time to light and arrange it properly.

If it is a large object such as an automobile or boat, decide which feature or quality you want to stress. Strong light will make the most of bright colors and reflective surfaces, as right. A low, three-quarter view exaggerates the size of the hood and front wheels. A 28 mm lens would have increased the perspective distortion. A higher viewpoint from the side, coupled with the dominant horizontals in the background, emphasizes the sleek, low lines of the car, below. A greased filter was used, below right, to make highlights sparkle.

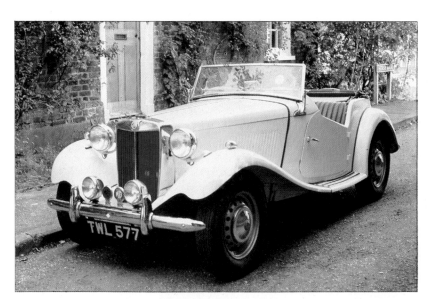

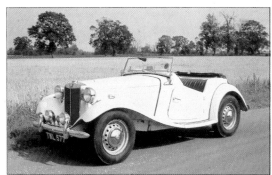

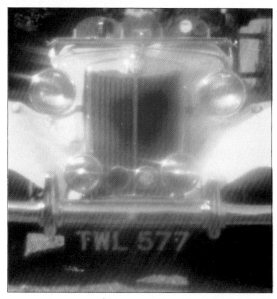

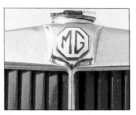

Focusing on detail
Use a telephoto or get right in close to pick out a detail, such as the insignia, left. Or choose from the range of close-up lenses and equipment available (p.56). Frame your subject so that lines and shapes make an interesting pattern.

Photographing a room

Shooting a room interior gives you maximum control over your subject. You can rearrange furniture and change the lighting by partially drawing blinds or curtains or by using strategically placed spotlights to illuminate objects of interest. Don't attempt to record the whole room – concentrate on an attractive corner or wall, as right and below, making sure that verticals line up with the sides of your frame. Both these pictures were taken from the same viewpoint, but a standard lens was used for the shot below, and a 28 mm lens for the shot right. Use the broader field of view of a wide-angle lens when you want to get more of an interior into your shot.

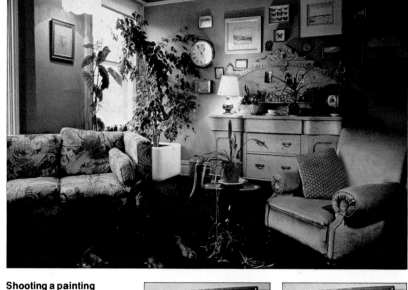

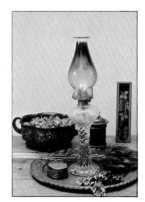

Shooting a painting

When photographing a painting, in a gallery or at home, use a polarizing filter to help eliminate reflections. Attach the filter to your lens and rotate it until the reflection disappears.

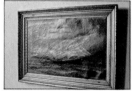

Setting up a still life

Photograph a collection of treasured possessions from around the home or of natural objects that you have found outside. Decide on a theme for your still life, choosing objects that complement one another in coloring, texture, and shape. And find a neutrally colored background that shows off your collection to advantage. Use fairly bright, even lighting and slow film to bring out fine detail. You will want to maximize depth of field, so stop down to your smallest aperture and use a slow shutter speed, with your camera mounted on a tripod. The objects shown in the sequence right were selected for their exotic, mysterious qualities and their harmonious colors.

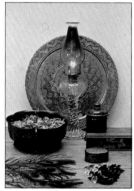

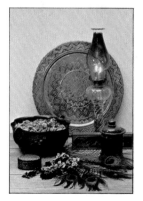

1 The objects have potential as a group, but colors and textures have been clumsily combined. Some of the objects are half-hidden and the centrally placed lamp dominates the composition.

2 The still life is beginning to take shape. The tray is well displayed at the back, with the lamp in front of it. But the small objects at the front are scattered and some lead the eye out of the frame.

3 The final version shows most unity. Smaller objects are well related at the front, while the bowl and blue pot now balance the tray. Moving the lamp off-center has strengthened the composition.

Weather and natural elements

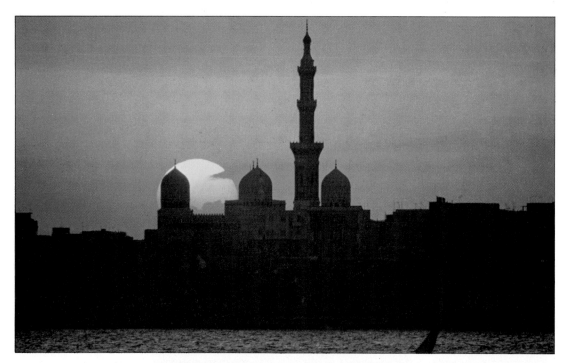

Many people put away their cameras when the sun goes down or the weather seems hostile. But it is often at these times that you find the most stunning effects of color and light. Be sure to bracket your exposures when light is failing or variable, as in storms. The setting sun is magnified by a 200 mm lens, above. as it sets behind an oriental skyline. (Never look through the viewfinder at the sun when it is high in the sky.) Shooting at dusk enabled the photographer to capture the eerie moonlit scene, right, with a slow shutter speed (1/15 sec).

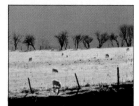

Stormy weather
In stormy weather, the dramatic light changes will transform both the mood and appearance of landscape, above. Here, a shaft of sun highlights the grassy slope, producing striking color contrast with the shadowed valley.

Clouds and skies

Unusual cloud formations and colorful skies can make exciting subjects in their own right. Notice how the photographer has composed the picture, right, according to the rule of thirds (p.28). Placing the cloud in the lower right-hand corner allows the fan-shaped rays of sunlight to spread out over the rest of the frame. Exposure was read from the blue sky alone, being a mid-tone between dark and light parts of the cloud. In the picture below, a 28 mm lens was used to accentuate the broad sweep of the sky.

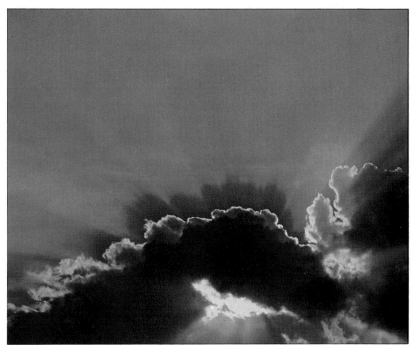

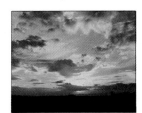

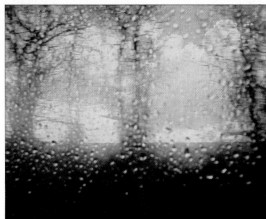

Muting colors

Haze, fog, rain, and flying sand all diffuse light, creating soft colors and shapes and a romantic or mysterious mood. A desert storm shrouds the figures in sand, above, subduing the colors of their clothes. The rain-spattered window, above right, has distorted the ghostly black trees outside, producing a subtle pattern of blues and blacks.

● Always protect your equipment well in such adverse conditions. Use a hood and a UV filter to keep water or sand off the lens (p.25).

Snow and frost

Close-ups of frosty details, like the strands of wool, left, often evoke the icy feel of winter better than distant snow scenes. Use side-lighting to reveal texture and expose for the bright detail itself, so that the background goes black.

Buildings and cityscapes

When shooting a building, take time to consider how you can bring out its most impressive features. Don't be content with your first view – walk around and observe the building from various angles. A head-on view, for instance, will reveal pattern; shooting a building through an arch or window will add a sense of depth (p.29). If possible, study your subject at different times of day. Use the hard shadows created by side-lighting to define structure, particularly with modern architecture.

Shooting from above
Try using a wide-angle lens from a high viewpoint to encompass a panoramic city view, as right. Notice how tilting the camera down has made the skyscrapers lean in toward the bottom. To prevent this, you must hold the camera level.

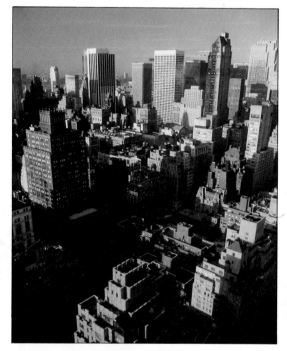

Using back-lighting
Chimneys and cranes are not the most attractive subject matter at first sight. But shooting into the light at sunset (and exposing for the sky) has made the most of their strong shapes by throwing them into silhouette.

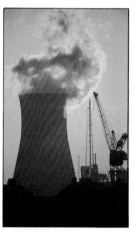

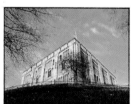

Shooting from below
Shooting a building from a close, low viewpoint distorts its shape, making the walls lean in at the top. The castle keep, above, has been reduced to a triangle against the sky. Warm evening sunlight has made the stonework glow.

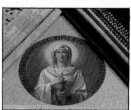

Using a telephoto lens
A telephoto lens is invaluable when you want to fill the frame with decorative details that would be inaccessible with a standard lens, as above. Make sure that your meter is reading for the detail itself (p.19).

People and views
Including a member of your family in a shot of a famous place is a perfect way of recording your visit. If you intend the place itself to be the main subject, don't allow the person to dominate, as top right. Position her farther away from the camera, at one side of the frame, as in the picture bottom right. If the person looks at the building, rather than the camera, it will help to draw attention to the point of interest.

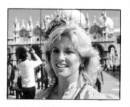
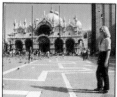

Using double perspective
Shooting a building from an oblique angle allows you to take advantage of double perspective. In the picture right, it has made the two walls of the castle recede sharply into the distance, giving a strongly three-dimensional image.

Interior details
Look for unusual ways of portraying details of a building's interior. The fascinating spiral pattern, below, was achieved by standing at the foot of the stairs and pointing the camera up at the ceiling, using the wrist strap (p. 14).

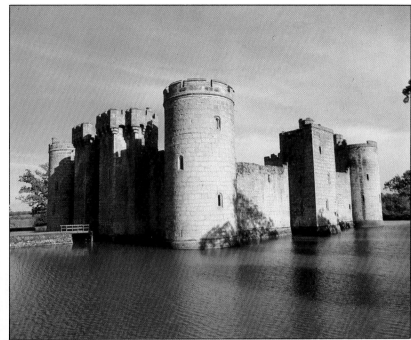

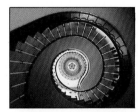

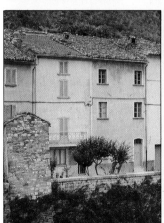

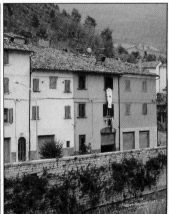

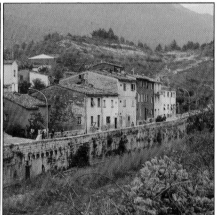

Making a panorama
Use either print or slide film (to be made into prints) to shoot a view that is too wide to fit the frame. Stand in one spot and take about four shots. Use verticals and horizontals as guides and overlap each by about one-third.

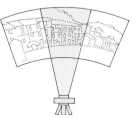

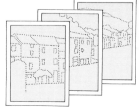

Arrange the finished prints in the correct order. Trim off overlapping areas (if any). Link up the connecting verticals and horizontals in the pictures and stick the completed panorama in your album.

Landscapes–depth and scale

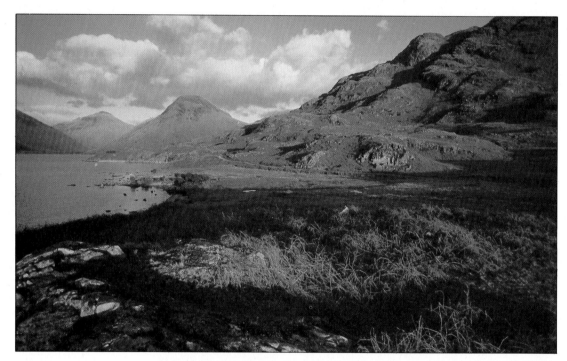

To take strong landscapes, you must develop an eye for the effects of light, weather and season, and a skill in conveying distance through viewpoint and composition. Mist and haze will mute colors and create a sense of mystery. Storms produce dramatic light changes – low clouds sweep across the sky, dappling the land with dense shadows and brilliant highlights, as above. For maximum sharpness in a distant view, set focus at 15–20 ft (4.5–6 m) and use a small aperture. Focusing for infinity may put the foreground out of focus.

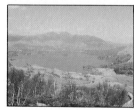

Be selective
Try not to clutter your landscapes with too much detail, as above. Select part of the scene with a strong focal point, as in the 80 mm lens shot right. And, if the sky is dull or pale, consider excluding it from the picture altogether.

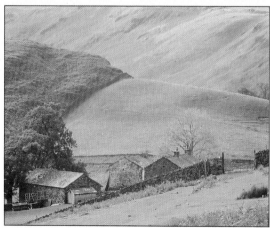

Lenses for landscape

Some types of scenery demand the special qualities of a wide-angle or telephoto lens. A 28 or 35 mm lens is ideal for a panoramic view, right. It includes more foreground, makes distant elements appear farther away, and steepens perspective. And its extreme depth of field gives sharp focus from fore- to background. Conversely, a 135 or 200 mm lens enlarges distant elements. It makes a far-off mountain look high and close, as below, and by picking out distant scenes, appears to compress subject planes, as below right. Its narrow depth of field puts fore- and background out of focus, softening colors.

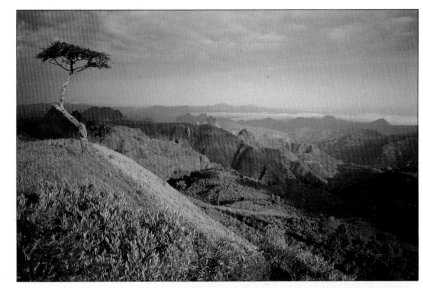

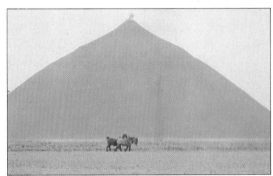

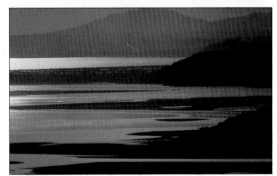

Depth and distance

Landscapes often prove to be disappointing in photographs because they lack the illusion of depth. Try to find a way of linking the foreground with the background. Make use of undulating or diagonal lines and shapes to draw the eye back, as in the pictures right. Better still, place a strong shape in the foreground to frame the view and indicate distance by its relative size, as far right.

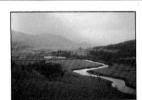

Other ways to imply depth

Shooting parallel lines as they converge into the distance, shooting through an open gateway, or putting a figure in the foreground looking at the view, will also suggest depth. A wide-angle lens increases the effect.

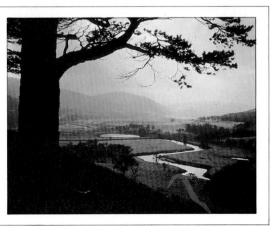

Outdoor activities and groups

Pictures taken on daytrips and outings form a unique record – you can't go back for more. Take plenty of film – including fast film and flash if the event is likely to run into the evening, and a variety of lenses to give you more scope (see facing page). Try to build a picture story of the whole day. Candid shots of the trip out and back and humorous incidents are as important as views of the setting. Make sure you have pictures of each occurrence and of everyone present, yourself included (p.76). The shots on this page were taken on a river picnic. The view from the landing stage, right, shows the milling pattern of boats and conveys the lazy river atmosphere. The shots on the facing page were taken at a country fair.

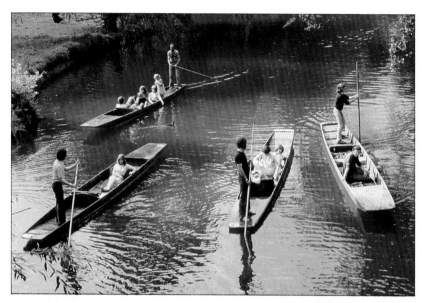

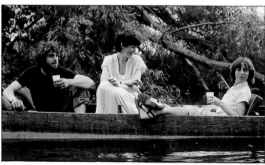

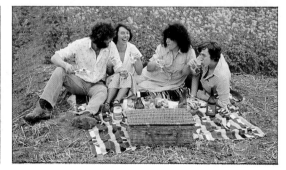

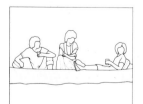

Arranging group shots
When you take shots of a group of people, your pictures will be stronger if you use part of the setting to provide a frame, as above. The line of the boat links the figures together, as shown left. Alternatively, you can arrange people around a center of interest, as in the picnic shot, above. The figures form a semicircle around the hamper, as shown right. Try to get heads at different levels and make sure that all the faces are visible. Wait for people to relax again before you shoot.

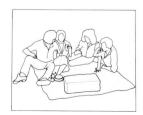

Using different lenses

Outdoor events offer far more picture-taking opportunities if you use different lenses. A long, 135mm, lens enabled the photographer to pick out individual members of the band, right and below right. Notice how its shallow depth of field has softened background colors. By contrast, a 28 mm wide-angle lens encompasses the whole band and much of the surrounding area in the two pictures below. Sharp focus now extends all the way from the foreground to the background.

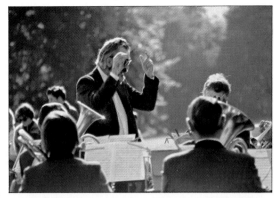

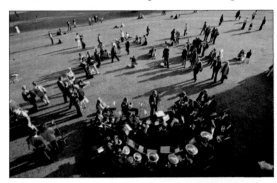

Getting up high

Choose your viewpoint with care. A shot from ground level, right, shows band and audience as a single mass. The high viewpoint, above, brings out the tight semicircle of the band and separates them clearly from the spectators.

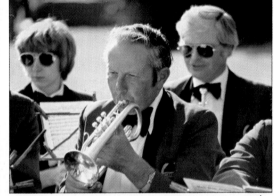

Spectator events

When shooting events that include performers and spectators, don't forget to turn your camera on the audience. Their attention will be absorbed, allowing you to shoot freely without being observed. A 200 mm lens picked out the engaging row of children's faces, right.

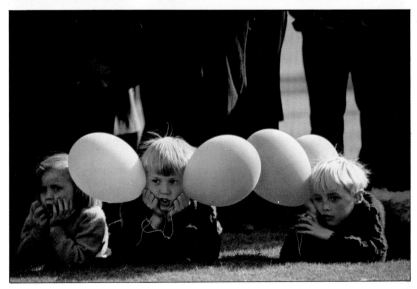

Indoor parties and celebrations

When photographing a special occasion, such as a Christmas party, try to record as many different aspects of the scene as you can. To capture the spirit of the occasion, use 400 ASA film (uprated if necessary) and shoot by existing light, rather than using flash, which will tend to destroy the mood. Go for the natural effect of a mixture of room lights and candle light, adding extra lamps to brighten any dark corners. On print film, this lighting combination will produce an acceptable warm cast, but slides may look too yellow. You can compensate for this by using tungsten film or, with daylight film, a color correcting filter (p.88).

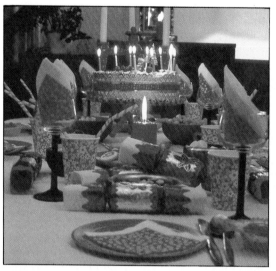

The festive spread
Photograph the table laden with food before people sit down. Shoot along the surface of the table to exaggerate perspective.

Shooting candle light
Reduce the room lights, but don't turn them all off unless you are prepared to give a very long exposure. Choose a low viewpoint to set the flames off against a dark background.

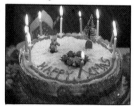

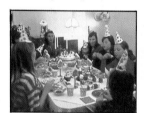

Photographing groups
When everyone has sat down, set up your equipment, choosing a camera position that gives a clear view of the whole group. If you can't get back far enough to include all you want, use a 28 mm lens – but take care to avoid distorting faces near the camera (p.46). When you are ready, attract people's attention and try to make them smile, right. If you catch them unawares, as above, your results may be disappointing.

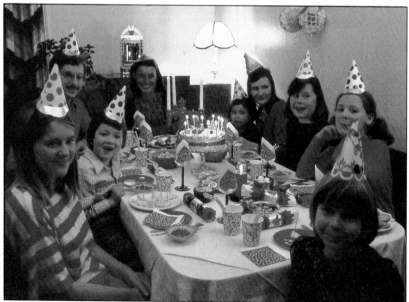

Humorous portraits
Take some candid shots of people while they are eating and drinking, as below, or pulling party crackers, right. Set focus and exposure in advance so that you are ready to press the shutter quickly and record expressions.

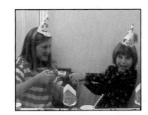

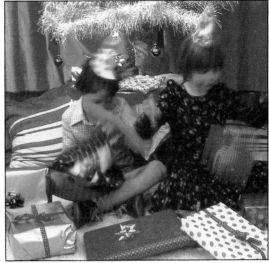

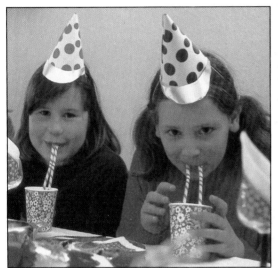

Blur for effect
You may capture the excitement of children opening presents more effectively by using a slow shutter speed and allowing their movement to blur, as above. The picture left looks contrived and stilted by comparison.

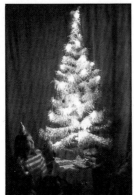

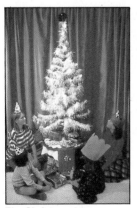

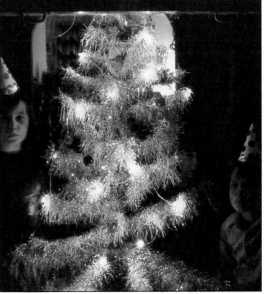

The Christmas tree
Try different ways of lighting a group around the lit-up tree. Room lights, above left, will record the scene in great detail. But your shot will have more atmosphere if you rely on the tree lights, above right, using a long exposure and a tripod. (Only faces nearest the tree will be well lit.) Or shoot the tree from outside, right, to frame the lights in a dark setting.

Theaters, circuses and shows

The brilliant costumes and lighting of stage shows provide a rich source of colorful subjects for photography. Always ask permission if you want to use your camera during a performance – it is usually granted at circuses, but may be hard to obtain at commercial theaters or concert halls. Try to see the show through once before taking any pictures so that you can make a note of the best moments to record. Shoot by available light, using 400 ASA film, or, if taking slides, tungsten light film, uprated. Flash is not effective unless used at close range and is usually prohibited anyway. Always bracket your shots, since it can be difficult to measure exposure accurately.

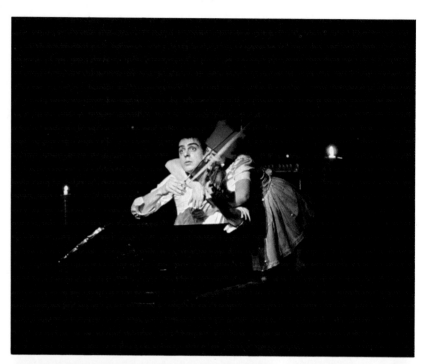

At the theater
When shooting a play, ballet or opera, aim to sit on a level with, or slightly above, the stage. You will find it easiest to expose accurately when the whole stage is well lit – take some shots of the entire cast, choosing a moment when their grouping is expressive. If you want to shoot two or three spotlit figures, as above, you will find it harder to obtain correct exposure. A good tip is to take a light reading when the whole stage is illuminated and keep to the same setting.

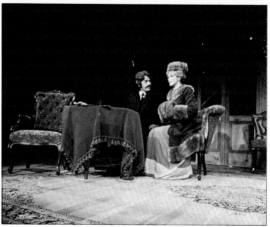

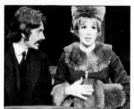

Standard or telephoto?
Use a standard lens to show characters in their setting, as left. But when you want to focus attention on facial expressions or costume detail, you will require the extra magnification of a telephoto lens, above.

At the circus
Try to get a seat a few rows from the edge of the ring, preferably by an aisle, so that you can move higher, if desired. For high-wire balancing and trapeze acts, you will find a telephoto lens an asset. The trapeze act, right, was shot on 160 ASA tungsten light film, uprated to 800 ASA to allow a shutter speed fast enough to freeze action. Subject colors are true to life but the overall effect is a little grainy and contrasty due to uprating. Daylight film has produced a warm, yellow cast in the trick-cycling shot, below. Including the silhouetted heads of the audience has recreated the feeling of being part of the occasion.

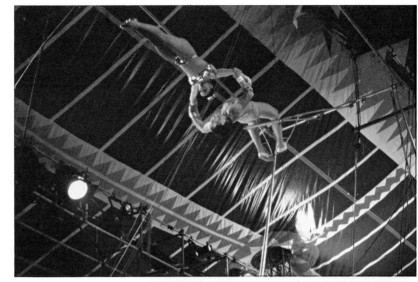

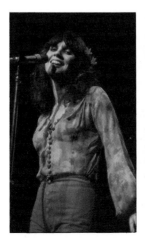

Catching the moment
Clowns, acrobats, and other ground-level performers are the easiest subjects to take at the circus. But it still helps if you have already seen the show, so that you can anticipate when the action will reach its peak. Perfect timing was essential to capture the expressive moment right.

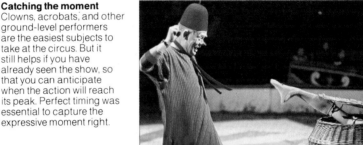

Singers and rock groups
At rock concerts, you can often move around and change position without difficulty. For shots of a band on stage, get back far enough to include all the musicians. But when photographing a solo singer, move right up to the front and shoot from just below the stage. From such close range, you will have more chance of gauging exposure correctly for the variable colored lighting. The pictures right were taken from very near the stage – the photographer was close enough to catch the singer's eye.

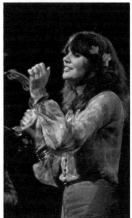

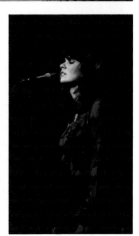

Vacations and travel

A vacation is a favorite time for photography, so make sure you have everything you need with you. Take:
- Plenty of film – fast for night shots : slow if you expect very bright sun
- Flash equipment
- Skylight or UV filter (p.88)
- Lens cap
- Lens hood to prevent sunlight causing flare
- Camera case and strap
- Camera equipment bag to protect everything

At airports keep film in your hand luggage – X-ray security checks can cause film to fog.

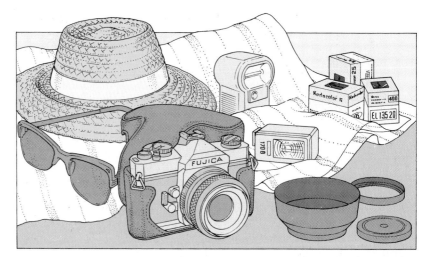

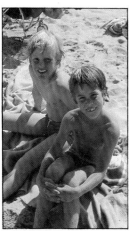

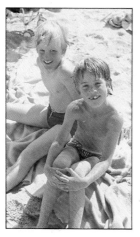

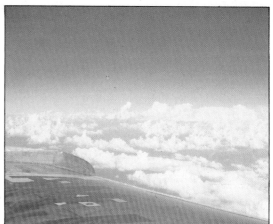

Exposure in bright sun
Glare from sand and water may mislead your meter into underexposing the main subject, as above. To get subject detail, as above right, read exposure from the main subject only (in this case from the face).

Using a self timer
A self timer enables you to include yourself in a group shot, as shown right. Find a firm camera support and preset focus and exposure. The self timer will fire the shutter about ten seconds after being set, giving you time to join the group.

Shooting on the move
When shooting from a moving vehicle, above, use a fast shutter speed to compensate for vibrations and prevent blur. Hold the camera near (but not touching) the window to avoid reflections, and set focus at 15–20 ft (5–6.5 m).

Recording your trip

Make the most of your vacation by keeping your camera with you at all times. Try to record the key moments and activities of your trip: picnics on the beach, hiking, sunbathing, games on the sand and in the water. Don't forget to take shots of your hotel or guest house and your favorite restaurant. When taking people in the sea, squat down at the water's edge and keep the camera low. In general restrict your beach shots to the morning or afternoon. Overhead sun at midday gives short ugly shadows. Use a skylight filter for all beach pictures if you want to reduce haze. Above all, be imaginative in your approach – turn the camera on fellow photographers or on the family's shadows on a sunlit rock face.
● Always load and unload film in the shade.

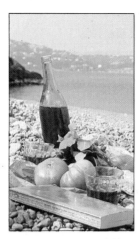
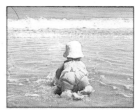
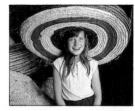
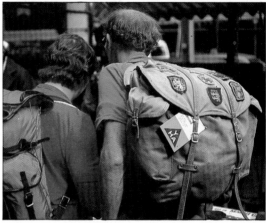
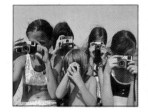
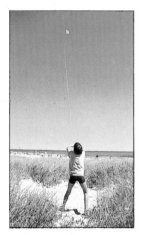
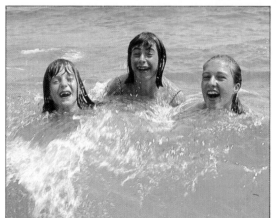
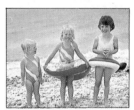
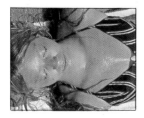
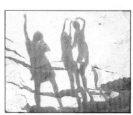
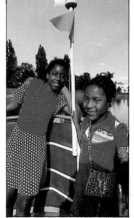

Seascapes and beaches

The elements of sand, sea, sun, and sky make exciting picture-taking material. On the beach you will mostly be working in very bright conditions, so consider using slow film or a neutral density filter (p.88) to allow a greater range of exposure settings. And always bracket your beach shots, as glare from water and sand may upset your meter reading. When capturing waves breaking, as right, get down low and choose a fast shutter speed (here 1/250 sec) to freeze motion. A skylight filter was used to reduce haze.

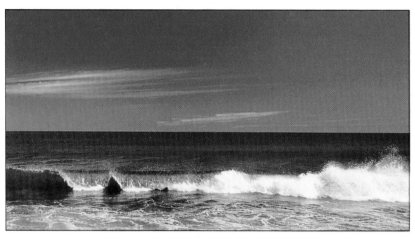

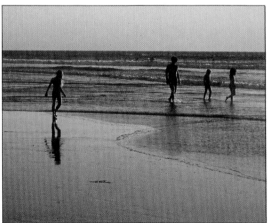

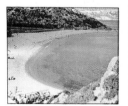
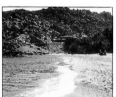
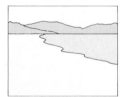
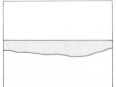

Using reflections
Reflections in wet sand, as above, or water, as right, enliven the foreground and make an interesting picture out of the simplest subject. When shooting perfect mirror images, make sure that you include the whole of the reflection.

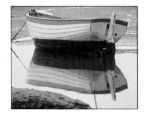

Beaches
When you are shooting a memorable beach, avoid bad results by getting up high and including some foreground interest. (Compare the shot and diagram above.)

When shooting from the beach, take care over dominant lines. A shot looking out to sea (diagram) would be dull. Shooting along the shoreline produces a lead-in connecting fore- and background.

Light on water

Notice how the direction of sunlight can change the appearance of a stretch of water – making it look flat and dull one moment, lively and sparkling the next. In general, low, oblique light will bring out the textured surface of the water, while back- and front-lighting will make it look calm. In the picture right, back-lighting at dusk has given the water the appearance of molten metal. Open expanses of water can lack impact – try moving back to include an object in the foreground. Here the palm trees give the picture depth and a stronger sense of location. Exposing for highlights (p.19) will help you to capture the shimmering quality of the water, while throwing foreground shapes into dramatic silhouette.

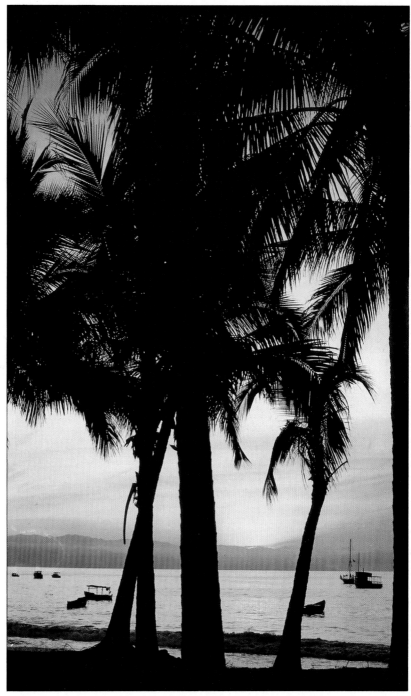

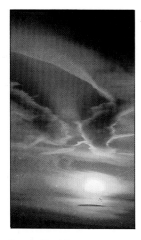

Dramatic skies

If the sky is unusually striking and colorful, as above, make it the subject of your picture. You will find skies at their most colorful and dramatic before sunset and during stormy weather. Take care to read exposure for the sky.

Individual sports

Exciting sports pictures are the result of careful planning, dedication, and, above all, fast timing. With sports like high jump or diving, you need quick reflexes to catch the moment when an action reaches its peak. In other activities, like gymnastics or dancing, you can take advantage of repeated or predictable patterns of movement to select an expressive image. For any sport, look out for typical actions and postures that show effort and skill.

Capturing the action
When shooting sports, you may find it hard to get close enough to the action, unless you use a telephoto lens. If you are a real sports enthusiast, it may be worth buying a lens of at least 200 mm, as used for the picture right. A fast shutter speed (1/500 sec) froze the tennis star's dramatic dive for the ball.

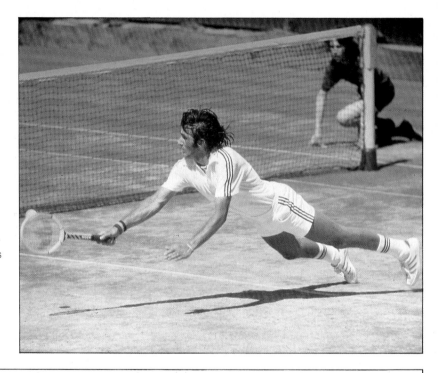

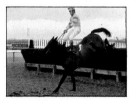 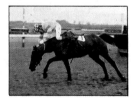 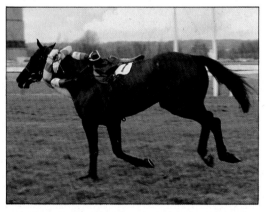

Using an autowinder
An autowinder (p.89) or motor drive allows you to shoot almost continuously, without pausing to wind on. You can take a rapid sequence of shots to cover consecutive stages of an action. Here, the photographer moved the camera slightly between shots to keep the horse in the frame. To produce a strong sequence, you may have to edit your shots – here three were chosen from a possible five.

Canoeing

Try to approach an outdoor hobby like canoeing from a variety of different angles. The photographer got broadside on to his subject, right, and caught him off-balance. Using a 28 mm lens has contributed a sense of depth to the shot. Zooming with an 85–200 mm lens (p.31) created a more dynamic effect in the picture far right. The radiating streaks of color simulate fast forward movement. Protect your camera well for watersports.

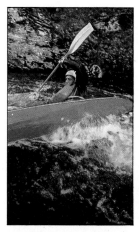

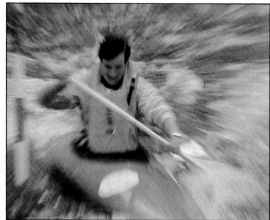

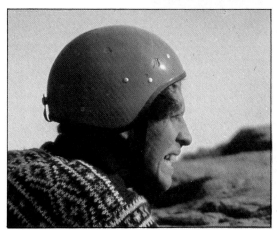

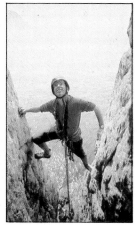

Rock-climbing

Move in close with a telephoto lens, as far left, to show individual effort and skill. The grim determination on the man's face eloquently conveys the precariousness of his position. But when you want to include your subject's surroundings, choose a wide-angle lens to gain sharp focus from foreground to background, as in the spectacular picture left. The scale of the distant view suggests the altitude of the climb. Exposing for shadows (p.19) has bleached out the sea and sky.

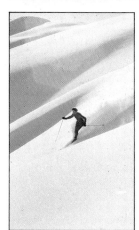

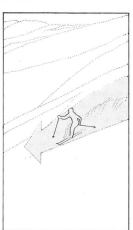

Skiing

For winter sports, lighting is usually bright enough to allow brief exposures. When choosing a shutter speed for a skier, take distance and direction of movement into account, as well as speed (p.30). Notice how the dominant diagonal lines (p.29), outlined in the diagram, and the flurry of snow give a powerful sense of the skier's movement, far left. For the slalom picture right, the photographer prefocused, read exposure from his hand, and pressed the shutter the instant the boy entered the point of focus.

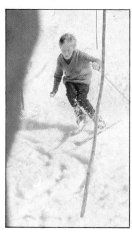

Team, track, and field sports

When photographing team events, plan to convey the particular characteristics of the sport, as well as its energy and excitement. Knowledge of the sport is invaluable in helping you to anticipate moments of climax in the action and plan the best locations to shoot from. Much of the time the action will be out of reach. Don't be tempted to move around and follow it, nor to shoot from too far away. Stay where you are and wait until the action passes close by. Or use a telephoto lens to bring it closer. Always use fast film, and shoot in bright sunlight, if you require shutter speeds fast enough to freeze motion.

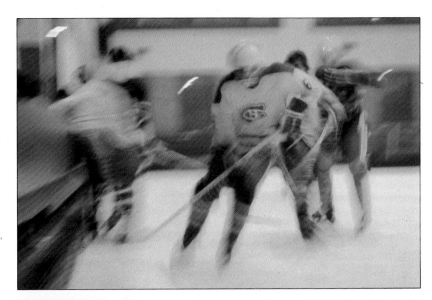

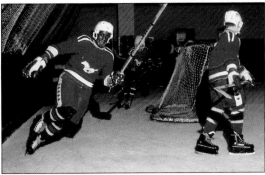

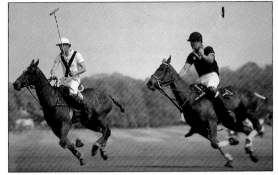

Indoor sports
Lighting in sports stadiums is seldom bright enough to allow a fast shutter speed, even with 400 ASA film. When you want to freeze action, you must use flash. In the picture above, flash has stopped the player in mid turn and recorded color and detail accurately. If you must rely on available lighting, try letting the action blur with a slow shutter to convey the speed of the game, as in the top shot. Notice how fluorescent lamps have added a cool greenish cast to the picture (p. 17).

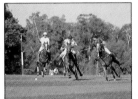

Isolating the subject
When shooting outdoor sports, look for a way of clearing the background. The trees and tight huddle of players, left, form a confused image. Isolating just two players against the sky, above, produces a picture with more impact.

Panning for effect
At track events, try panning the camera to get your subject sharp and make it stand out from a nondescript or distracting background. Using a telephoto lens will further isolate the subject, but you must use a tripod and pan head. The picture, right, was taken with a 200 mm lens, panned at 1/60 sec – a relatively short exposure. Notice how the background is reduced to a soft blur of color, while sharp detail is shown on the car.

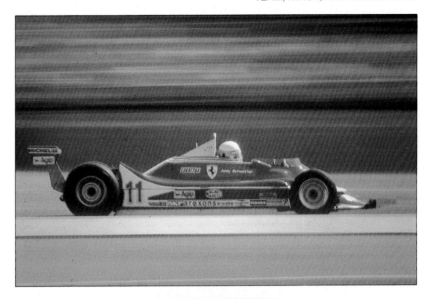

Using a prism lens
A prism lens provides an effective way of filling the frame from a distance. This multifaceted lens attachment, shown far right, screws on to the front of the lens, like a filter. It produces one central image of a subject, surrounded by fainter repeat images. In the picture right, it has created a sense of the competitiveness of the event, from one single car. Other types of prism lens produce multiple images that repeat horizontally across the frame, and convey a sense of speed.

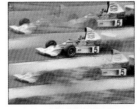
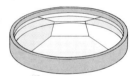

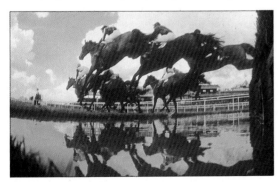

Lens and viewpoint
A range of focal lengths enables you to portray different aspects of a sporting event. At a steeplechase, use a low viewpoint beside one of the jumps for a dramatic wide-angle shot, as above. The photographer chose a 21 mm lens at 1/500 sec to exaggerate the feeling of movement. Or look for a clear view of a corner and use a telephoto lens, prefocused on the rail, to bunch the horses together as they come round the bend, as in the 200 mm shot, right.

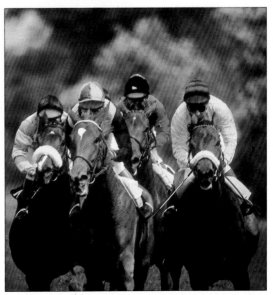

Ordering prints/Faults

There is a wide variety of printing services on the market. The chart, right, shows what the main ones offer and how costs compare. Many services provide a range of surface finishes – the most common are mat, glossy and luster. And most don't charge for any picture that fails to print. The main advantage of the costlier services is that they assess each negative individually, which allows for exposure variation and gives superior quality. And they will enlarge a part of the negative. To order an enlargement from part of the negative only, mask the negative with tracing paper and indicate the exact area that you would like to have enlarged.

Service	How to find it	What it offers	Quality	Cost	Speed
Mail order	Magazine advertisement Postal mailings	Standard print size – 5 × 3½ in from 35 mm	Prints bulk-processed Quality fluctuates Difficult to complain	Cheapest, but credit systems can commit you and/or make it more costly	Usually about one week, depending on mail service
Local photo or drug store	Main street	Same as above	Same variable quality as above, but possible to complain	Cheap	Quick, usually 3–5 days
Amateur photo lab	Photographic magazines	Will print any size Most provide print-from-slide service	Good quality and service	More costly Economic price-offers for whole-neg enlargement, only × 7	Quick, usually 5 days
Pro-fessional lab	Phone book or trade directory	Same as above	Very good quality Specialized service	Most expensive, but gives free contacts – you specify what enlargements you want	Very quick, 24 hours or less if required

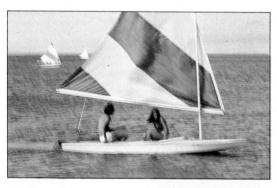

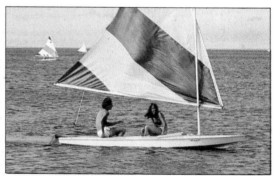

Choosing a print for enlargement

Among your prints there may be several that you would like to enlarge further. But, to enlarge well, a shot must be very sharp, and you can only judge this from the negative, not from the resulting print.

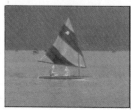

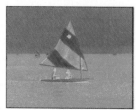

Both the negatives shown left would give reasonable standard-sized prints. But when part of each negative is enlarged by several times, the difference is obvious. So when choosing a shot, always examine the negative for sharpness with a magnifying glass.

Using the camera
- **Subject "bleached out"**
  Don't use direct flash too
  near subject (p.21).
  Diffuse flash when
  working close up (p.35)
- **Camera let in light**
  Make sure camera back
  is properly closed while
  film is in camera (p.9)
- **Film loaded twice**
  When unloading film,
  wind film tongue back
  into cassette. Mark
  clearly any films you
  have already exposed

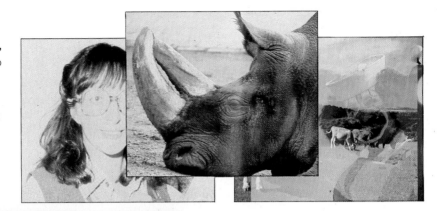

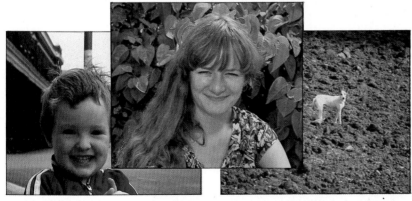

Taking the picture
- **Cluttered background**
  Look around frame and
  beyond main subject to
  check background is
  clear of distracting
  objects (p.27)
- **Person squinting**
  For portraits, make sure
  subject is not looking
  directly into sun (p.47)
- **Subject too far away**
  Consider main subject's
  size in relation to frame.
  Move in close to exclude
  anything extraneous (p.27)

Processing and handling
- **Dust on negative**
  Negatives carelessly
  handled at processors.
  Send film back and
  complain
- **Strong color cast**
  Processor has used
  wrong filtering.
  Send film back and
  complain
- **Film affected by heat**
  Never leave film or
  camera in hot place,
  glove pocket or back
  shelf of automobile

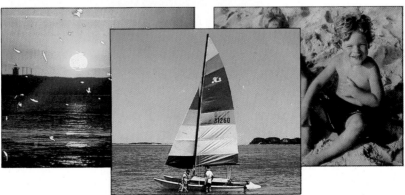

Presenting prints

If you are pleased with the pictures you have taken, it's worth spending a little time and money on displaying them well.

Building up an album

The ideal way of displaying your best prints is in an album. Make the best possible use of the page and try to avoid wasting space. as near right. First. sort the prints out into logical sequences. Then juggle them around on the page until you find an attractive layout. as far right. Mix print sizes and formats and consider how the colors and shapes in your shots relate to one another. If the album has dark pages, use self-adhesive labels for captioning.

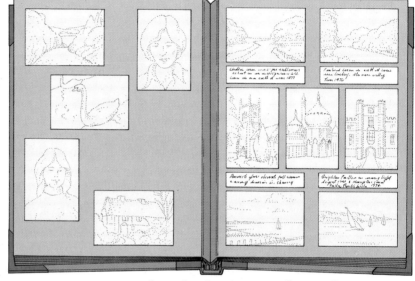

Mounting album prints

Some albums have ready-made methods for holding prints. such as self-adhesive pages with a cling-plastic overlay. **1**. or slit corners. **2**, which take standard prints only.

If your album has plain pages, you can, **3**, mount prints with double-sided adhesive or rubber cement. Or use opaque, **4**, or transparent, **5**, self-adhesive corners.

Dry mounting

Use the dry mounting method to mount larger prints. Attach a piece of shellac tissue to the center back of your print, using a cool iron. Trim off excess tissue and position the print carefully on the card mount. Hold it in place while you iron the tissue to the mount at all four corners. Then cover the print with a piece of thin card and iron the whole print, pressing firmly.

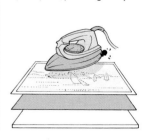

Displaying your prints

Use this list to help you choose from the vast array of print display methods on the market.

1 Traditional album – the best way of displaying a large collection of prints

2 Double-sided photo frame for twin portraits

3 Plastic frame in various different sizes

4 Decorative silver frame – costly, but best for a romantic portrait or wedding shot

5 Wood-rimmed frame with glass – various sizes

6 Mini album with slip-in plastic sleeves – for carrying in pocket or bag

7 Your personal greeting card – made by dry mounting a favorite print on a folded piece of card

8 Pocket album with slip-in plastic sleeves – prints inserted back to back

9 Plastic cube – displays five prints simultaneously

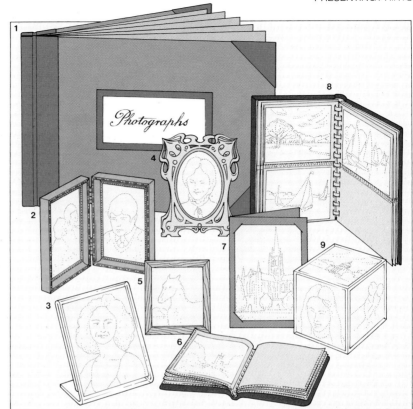

Showing slides

If you use slide film, it is worth buying a projector and screen to show them. Projecting slides brings out their brilliant colors and enlarges your shots almost to life size. There is a wide variety of projectors available, ranging from cheap, hand-operated models to more advanced types, like the projector right, that can change slide by remote control and focus automatically. If you can't afford a ready-made screen, improvise with a white, emulsion-painted wall or a large piece of mat, white cardboard. When planning a show, edit your slides, then arrange them in sequence in the projector tray. A hand viewer, right,is for previewing slides.

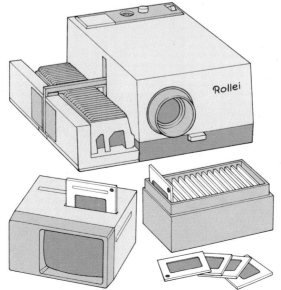

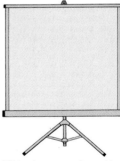

Slide storage and marking

Always store mounted slides in boxes or trays to protect them from damp and dust. Mark each mount in the bottom, left-hand corner, as shown left. Load your slides into the projector tray with the mark top right, facing the tray rear. They will then be projected the right way around.

Filters/Accessories/Zoom

Filters change a subject's appearance by altering the nature, quality, or color of light reaching the film. Some distort subject colors and shapes; others help to keep the image colors true. Most are made of glass mounted in a metal surround that screws into the lens. You can buy filters to fit lenses of most focal lengths.

● Use colored filters only with slide film – automatic processing will correct color casts on prints.

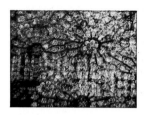

Colored prism filter
This creates multiple over-lapping images in rainbow colors. A bright subject on a dark background gives the best effect, as above.

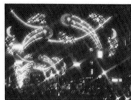

Cross-screen filter
This has a criss-cross grid that makes highlights look star-shaped. Use it for scenes with bright lights or reflections, as above.

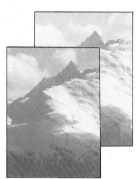

UV and skylight filters
These both help to neutralize the blue color cast, commonly found in snow scenes and when the sky is clear blue or overcast – the skylight filter by its pale pink color, the UV by absorbing UV light. They also improve the definition and color of distant views. Compare the pictures above – the front shot, taken with a skylight filter looks warmer and crisper.

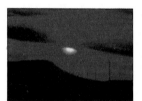

Colored filter
This adds a strong overall cast to a scene, as above. Many colors are available, in various strengths.

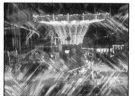

Diffraction filter
This is a colorless filter that splits or "diffracts" rays of light into bursts of rainbow colors, as above.

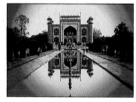

Spot filter
This colored filter with a clear middle surrounds a central subject with diffused color, as above.

Other useful filters	Effect
Neutral density (gray)	Reduces light, allowing wider apertures or longer exposures in bright light.
Polarizing (gray)	Darkens blue skies and reduces reflections from glass (p.63) and water.
80 A (blue)	Corrects color when you use daylight slide film in tungsten light.
Diffuser (colorless)	Spreads highlights and softens colors and shapes for a romantic effect.
Graduated (half-color)	Tints (or darkens) the sky half of landscapes.
Dual color (two tints)	Tints each half of the picture a contrasting color.

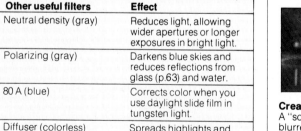

Creating soft focus
A "soft focus" or slightly blurred picture is often more evocative than a pin-sharp image. To create soft focus, you must diffuse the light entering the lens by using a diffuser (see left) or by improvising.

Smearing a thin layer of grease on a clear filter has blurred the lights, above left. Tying a nylon stocking over the lens has muted the colors and enhanced the soft texture of the petals in the flower shot, above.

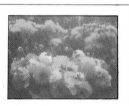

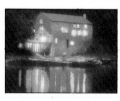

Useful accessories

1 A "gadget bag" with stiff sides and separate, padded compartments for camera, lenses, flash and films. As well as carrying all your equipment, it offers complete protection against knocks, jolts, dust, sand, and rain.

2 A soft, waterproof shoulder bag is a cheaper and lighter alternative. Line it with foam to cushion your equipment.

3 An "everready" case protects the camera but does not hold extra films or lenses. It may be supplied with the camera when you buy it.

4 A sturdy tripod holds the camera steady for long exposures (p.15). If possible, buy one with adjustable legs and a pan and tilt head so that you can position the camera at different heights and angles and pan it smoothly for action shots (p.31).

5 A cable release lets you fire the shutter without touching the camera (p.15).

6 A flash unit, connected to the camera's hot shoe, is useful for freezing action in dim light, brightening colors, and filling in shadows.

7 An autowinder or motor drive winds on automatically after you press the shutter. Some types allow you to shoot as many as five frames per sec.

8 A coiled extension lead connects your flash to your camera, enabling you to use your flash off-camera.

9 Metal or rubber lens hoods, for each focal length, reduce flare in bright sun and protect the lens from dust and rain.

10 A set of three extension tubes, used with a standard lens, enables you to record a close-up subject almost life-size (p.56).

11 A wide neck strap is a comfortable and steady way of carrying the camera, leaving your hands free.

12 A narrow, plaited neck strap is a cheaper alternative. But it slips off more easily and may let the camera swing about.

Zoom lens
A zoom lens has a special extra control, in addition to focusing and aperture rings, that alters its focal length. With a zoom, you can make the image larger or smaller without pausing to change lens or move your camera position. One zoom therefore takes the place of several lenses of fixed focal length, giving you the benefit of a range of focal lengths, without the inconvenience of

carrying a lot of extra equipment. No zoom lens at present spans the complete range of focal lengths from ultra wide-angle to extreme telephoto. One may be 35–70 mm, another 80–200 mm, and so on. Zooms are also larger and more expensive than fixed focus lenses and have smaller maximum apertures, making them of limited use in low available light.

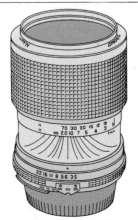

Using your zoom lens
Extend the lens to its longest focal length to measure exposure. The image will be larger in the frame, enabling you to take a selective reading, without moving closer. Likewise, if your zoom holds focus when you change focal length, focus with the lens fully extended. On some zooms, you alter focal length by rotating a ring. On others, as left, you slide the lens in or out, making zooming for effect (p. 31) easier.

Advanced and non-35 mm SLRs

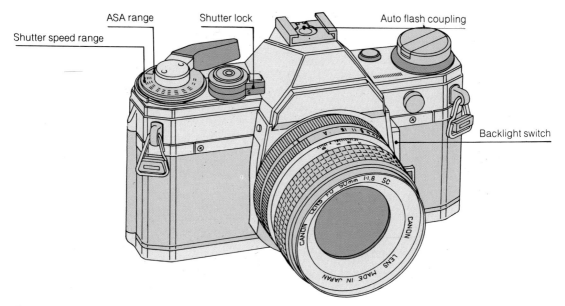

Shutter speed range

ASA range

Shutter lock

Auto flash coupling

Backlight switch

Typical advanced SLR features

The top end of the SLR market offers increasing sophistication and automation. But more advanced cameras also demand more technical knowhow, if you are to take full advantage of their complex controls. An advanced SLR camera may include any of the following features:

● **Quiet shutter release**
An electromagnetic shutter release button is very quiet. On the model above, it also turns on the metering system when pressed halfway down.

● **Shutter lock**
This prevents you pressing the shutter accidentally.

● **Shutter speed range**
The range of shutter speeds available is wider – on the model above, it extends from 1/1000 sec to 2 secs; on other models, from 1/2000 sec to as much as 30 secs.

● **ASA setting range**
The ASA dial can be set for a greater range of film speeds – on the model above, from 25–3200 ASA; on others, from 6–12000 ASA.

● **Eyepiece cover**
This covers the viewfinder to prevent stray light entering and biasing the meter reading.

● **Extra viewfinder data**
A typical viewfinder, below, includes an aperture scale, warning marks for overexposure, and LEDs that flash to indicate underexposure or remind you that the aperture ring is not set at "automatic".

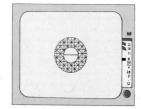

● **Auto flash**
Auto-coupling flash units automatically set the correct shutter speed and aperture for flash.

● **Interchangeable backs**
The camera back is often interchangeable – either for a data back, which prints the date on the corner of your negatives, or for a bulk film back, which holds as many as 250 frames of film.

● **Backlight control switch**
The switch, below, opens up the lens by 1½ stops when you press the shutter, to give correct exposure for backlit subjects.

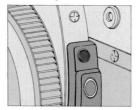

● **Multimode meter**
This offers a choice of four or five programmes for exposure measurement, including aperture priority, shutter speed priority, and manual.

● **Choice of metering**
This enables you to use an overall system for even lighting conditions, then switch to take a local spot reading from a distance in contrasty light.

● **Exposure memory lock**
This holds your exposure reading at a given setting, so that you can move up to your subject for a close-up reading, then use this setting to take a picture farther back.

● **Range of screens**
Interchangeable focusing screens are available for some models, to suit personal preference or special lenses, including clear field, center prism, grid, and plain.

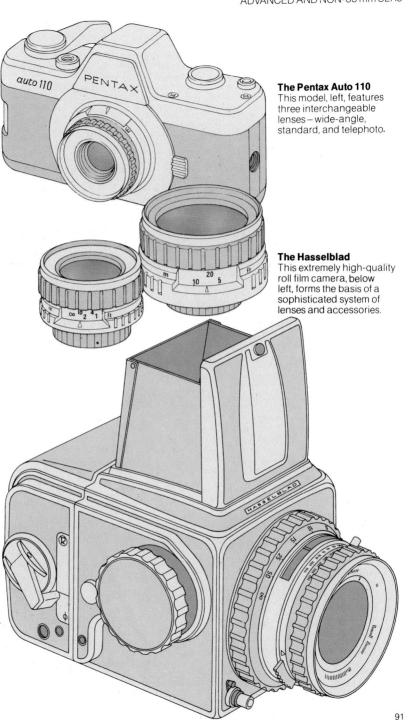

Small 110 SLRs

These cameras take 110 film cartridges, giving 11 × 17 mm negatives or slides. The cartridges are quick and easy to load, but only a limited range of films is available. The small negative size means that enlargements over about postcard size tend to show pronounced grain and loss of definition. The main advantage of these cameras is their lightness and compactness, making them a good choice for traveling. But their light weight also increases their tendency to camera shake. Only a few SLR cameras are currently available in the 110 format – Minolta makes a 110 SLR zoom with a limited choice of focal lengths, Pentax produces the Auto 110, shown right.

The Pentax Auto 110

This model, left, features three interchangeable lenses – wide-angle, standard, and telephoto.

The Hasselblad

This extremely high-quality roll film camera, below left, forms the basis of a sophisticated system of lenses and accessories.

Large, roll film SLRs

These cameras take roll film, giving slides or negatives in a square, or almost square, format – either 6 × 6 cm ($2\frac{1}{4}$ × $2\frac{1}{4}$ in), 6 × 7 cm, or 6 × 4.5 cm. These negative sizes produce very sharp enlargements, making a large format SLR ideal for still life and portrait photography. Loading a roll film camera takes more time than a 35 mm SLR – the film loads into a magazine which fits on to the back of the camera. Most models take interchangeable magazines; some also accept an instant picture film back. Large format SLRs are designed primarily for waist-level viewing and give a laterally reversed image. This can usually be corrected by fitting a pentaprism adaptor. They are bulkier and heavier than 35 mm SLRs and cost around five times as much.

Index

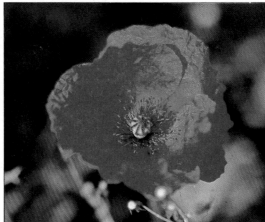

Acknowledgments

All photographs by Andrew de Lory except:
A. Bailey 77tl C. Boursnell 36bl, br D. Bradfield 11t; 12; 13t, c; 23 except bl, br; 26–7; 34; 35 except box; 46 box; 62–3; 72–3 J. Bulmer 2; 43; 64t; 66tr; 69 except box D. Burton 29br; 66bl J. Burton/B. Coleman 59tl A. Carroll 17c J. Cleare 4; 68t; 69 box; 81 except tr B. Coleman 92 G. Cranham 30t; 31cr; 80; 81tr; 83 C. Davis 48br L.R. Dawson/B. Coleman 57t A. le Garsmeur 67tr F. Herrmann 37bl, br S. King 75cl M. Langford 53cl; 65tr, b; 77tr, 2nd row l, 3rd row c R. Laurance 68br J. Loughran 48bl P. Loughran 57c, cr, bc D. Moreby 58bl, br M. Newton 29tl; 67 box D. Pearson 51tl; 68bl; 77tc, bc; 79r E. Pelham 18t, cl, cr; 21 box; 29cl; 44–5; 46 except box; 47; 54 except bl; 55; 60–1; 65tl; 70; 85c R. Perry 35 box t; 74 R. Pring 48t; 57bl E. Raff 41br; 64br; 65cl H. Reinhard/B. Coleman 56 J. Shaw/B. Coleman 57cl T. Stephens 76cr P. Tucker 50bl H. Wilkinson 49 J. Godfrey Wood 16t; 29cr; 39r; 40cl; 57br; 78cl, box

Dorling Kindersley and the author thank all the people who have helped to produce this book; including camera manufacturers and distributors (especially Agfa, Kodak and Olympus), Charles Elliott, Ian Carr, Harry Pepper, John Marshall of Smeets, Pelling and Cross Ltd., D.G. Leisure Centre
Illustrations by: Norman Lacey M.I.S.T.C.
Diagrams by: Gary Marsh
Photographic services by: Paulo Color and Negs
Typesetting services by: Contact Graphics and Alphabet
Origination services by: City Engraving
Props and locations by: London Contemporary Dance Theatre, Mishkenot Sha'ananim, Jerusalem, Guards Polo Club, MG Owners' Club